THE THEOPOLITAN VISION

THEOPOLIS FUNDAMENTALS
SERIES INTRODUCTION

The Theopolis Institute is a community of pastors, theologians, and students devoted to articulating and disseminating a vision of the church's mission to contemporary culture, a vision that centers on biblical theology and liturgical practice. The church carries on her world-transforming mission by being the church. When the church inhabits the symbolic world of the Bible through the liturgy, and communes together at the Lord's table, she becomes a source of light and life to the world.

Theopolis teaches, develops tools, and fosters networks to assist church leaders throughout the world to form thoroughly biblical, liturgical, and catholic churches. The Theopolis Institute is not a church, but is like scaffolding to assist the church in rebuilding God's heavenly city so that it can effectively carry out her mission of transforming the cities of man.

The Theopolis Institute was established in 2013, but its leaders have been working together to formulate and teach a Theopolitan vision of Bible, liturgy, church, and culture for several decades through James B. Jordan's Biblical Horizons.

The Theopolis Fundamentals Series introduces the Biblical Horizons / Theopolis outlook and agenda to a new generation. The early volumes of the series summarize our convictions about biblical interpretation, liturgical theology and practice, and the church's cultural and political mission. The Fundamentals will be followed by a collection of Theopolis Explorations volumes that will examine Scripture, liturgy, and culture in more depth and detail.

For more information about Theopolis, visit our web site at TheopolisInstitute.com.

THE THEOPOLITAN VISION

PETER J. LEITHART
PHD, UNIVERSITY OF CAMBRIDGE
PRESIDENT OF THEOPOLIS INSTITUTE

Theopolis
BOOKS
AN IMPRINT OF ATHANASIUS PRESS

The Theopolitan Vision
by Peter J. Leithart

Theopolis Books

Copyright © 2019 Theopolis Books
An Imprint of Athanasius Press

Athanasius Press
715 Cypress Street
West Monroe, Louisiana 71291
www.athanasiuspress.org

Cover design: Ryan Harrison
Typesetting: Christopher D. Kou

ISBN: 978-1-7335356-4-9

CONTENTS

ACKNOWLEDGEMENTS

I serve as President of the Theopolis Institute, a Christian think tank and training center based in Birmingham, Alabama. We teach, develop resources, and facilitate networks for men and women who share, or want to learn more about, the "Theopolitan vision" laid out in this book. For more information, see our web site, TheopolisInstitute.com.

I've had the help of a number of colleagues and friends. My oldest son, Woelke, used a part of his enforced vacation to proofread an earlier draft. My Theopolis colleagues Alastair Roberts and John Crawford read through the manuscript and made many helpful suggestions. Pastor Steve Jeffery of Emmanuel Church in north London gave his wise input, which I, foolishly, haven't always taken.

This is the first in a series of books, the "Theopolis Fundamentals," that lays out the Theopolitan vision in more detail. Future volumes will explore hermeneutics, liturgy, and culture, which are the Theopolis Institute's three zones of interest. I pray that this book, and the series it launches, will be a tool for building Christ's blessed city, the heavenly Salem, our vision dear of peace and love.

BLESSED CITY

1   Blessed city, heavenly Salem,
vision dear of peace and love,
who of living stones art builded
in the height of heaven above,
and with angel hosts encircled,
as a bride dost earthward move!

2   From celestial realms descending,
bridal glory round thee shed,
meet for him whose love espoused thee,
to thy Lord shalt thou be led;
all thy streets and all thy bulwarks
of pure gold are fashioned.

3   Bright thy gates of pearl are shining,
they are open evermore;
and by virtue of his merits
thither faithful souls do soar,
who for Christ's dear name in this world
pain and tribulation bore.

4   Many a blow and biting sculpture
polished well those stones elect,
in their places now compacted
by the heavenly Architect,
who therewith hath willed for ever
that his palace should be decked.

5   To this temple, where we call thee,
come, O Lord of Hosts, to-day;
with thy wonted loving-kindness
hear thy servants as they pray,
and thy fullest benediction
shed within its walls alway.

6   Here vouchsafe to all thy servants
what they ask of thee to gain,
what they gain from thee for ever
with the blessed to retain,
and hereafter in thy glory
evermore with thee to reign.

7   Laud and honour to the Father,
laud and honour to the Son,
laud and honour to the Spirit,
ever Three, and ever One,
consubstantial, co-eternal,
while unending ages run.

JOHN MASON NEALE

TO THE READER

I'm going to call you Theo or Thea.

"Theo" is the name we use at the Theopolis Institute to describe the kind of man who can most benefit from what we have to offer. "Thea" is the feminine version.

If you're Theo or Thea, you're young, or young-ish. You're an Evangelical Christian—that is, a Christian committed to the Bible. You may be a pastor or a seminary student. You may be a lay leader in the church, or a member observing from a distance.

Theo and Thea share a desire to follow Jesus and become more like Him, your interest in the Bible, your love for the church. These loves shape everything in your life.

You love the church's tradition, but you aren't a traditionalist. You realize that the church has to address the challenges of the present, but you aren't a progressive.

But Theo and Thea share something else: a restless hunger for something more.

If you're a pastor, you feel you're skimming the surface of the biblical text but don't know how to dig deeper. You know it's God's word, but you wonder why it's so weird. You may find yourself avoiding some biblical books (Leviticus, parts of Judges) and sticking to the clearer, safer bits, where you at least have *some* idea of what's going on.

If you're a layman or laywoman, you're edified by your pastor's sermons, but you suspect there's so much more to be said. You ask questions, but they don't get answered. You Google, but you're rightly cautious about what passes for theology on the Internet.

You attend worship at least once a week, but you wonder if there isn't more. You've slipped away in the last few months to attend an Anglican Evensong, and that somehow seems much more like worship. You know some churches have weekly communion. That seems intuitively right, though you're not sure why.

You sense there's something deeply wrong with today's world, and you're anxious for the future. But you don't want to turn the clock back, you don't want to stand with the doomsayers, and you think that the politicization of Christianity does more harm than good. Your skin crawls when other Christians merge Christian faith with patriotism. Your skin also crawls when Christians hitch their faith to the latest fad.

You know Jesus is the answer and that the church is called to carry on Jesus' ministry of healing, justice, salvation. You want to be part of something big, and Jesus' mission is as big as it gets. But you wonder if the church is up to the challenge.

You don't want to become Roman Catholic or Orthodox. You have Catholic and Orthodox friends, and you know they're Christians. Yet you don't buy the Papacy and don't want to venerate icons. Besides, your mother would roll in her grave if you swam the Tiber or moved to Constantinople.

You love your church. You love its vigor and its commitment to the Bible. You love its evangelistic fervor. But you're appalled at the divisiveness of Protestantism. You long for the church to be united.

Worst of all, you think you're the only one in the world who feels this way. You have coffee every other week with another pastor who shares your longings, but the two of you seem alone in the wilderness. You have a friend or two at church with whom you carry on whispered conversations about your restlessness.

You don't want to be divisive. You know that your pastor is responsible for you, and you want to honor him. You don't quite know what you want to be different. Only that you want something more. And you have trouble being patient.

Sound familiar? If so, you're Theo or Thea.

This book is for Theos and Theas, for pastors and laypeople, who are looking for something more. That more is what I'm calling the "Theopolitan vision."

What's that? This book will explain it as straightforwardly and simply as I can. But let me give you the gist right here.

The Theopolitan vision is a view of the church and her role in the world. I'm going to show that the church is an outpost of the future city of God. The city of God exists now, in the present, as a real-life society among the societies of men. This real-world, visible community is the family of the Father, the body of the Son, the temple of the Spirit. It exists to transform and renew human societies, inside and out, top to bottom. As God's city, the church carries out a global mission of urban renewal.

Worship is the primary work of God's city. Christian worship should be attuned to the liturgical tradition of the church, the whole church, but it should avoid traditionalism and nostalgia. Our practice and understanding of worship must be shaped by the whole Bible—from Genesis through Leviticus and Chronicles to Revelation. Worship should be saturated with Scripture—Scripture read, Scripture taught, Scripture sung, Scripture turned into a dialogue of love between the Lord and His Bride.

Worship is thinly Christian unless it culminates in joyous

festivity of the Lord's table. The liturgy is the place where we encounter the Word of God, where our worlds are shattered and rebuilt, where we learn to inhabit the symbolic universe of Scripture.

A church that worships biblically, a church whose worship is saturated by Scripture, a church whose members have learned to navigate biblically through life, a church that shares Christ's body and blood each week—*that* is a church prepared for mission.

The garden, the place of worship, is the source of the living water that flows to the world. The sanctuary is the beacon whose light shines out among the nations. Unless we taste the kingdom in worship—and I mean literally *taste*—we won't have the words of life that the world needs to hear. If we don't encounter the light of Jesus in His word and at His table, we won't be lights in the darkness.

Some Theos are pastors or aspiring pastors. If you're that kind of Theo, I commend you. Pastoral ministry isn't what you'd call a "sexy" profession. "A clergyman is nothing," says Mary Crawford in Jane Austen's *Mansfield Park*, and Mary Crawford knows a thing or two about sexiness.

As a pastor, you won't get rich. You won't win prestige. You won't gain attention unless you make a point of being provocative.

You'll grind away, week in and week out, teaching the Bible to more-or-less attentive parishioners, counseling, confronting, comforting. You'll spend an inordinate number of hours sharing the crisis moments of life—sickness, marital breakdown, wayward children, job losses. There's no reliable way to measure success. Your work may seem pointless, the results meager.

Yet you've chosen this vocation, or been chosen for it. I don't commend you for your willingness to accept obscurity. I commend you for believing that this vocation *matters*.

Because, despite widespread opinion, it *does*. It matters more than anything. A pastor at the pulpit is at the wheel of the ship of the world. A pastor offering the body and blood of Jesus at the Lord's table is at the center of the universe. A pastor leads the charge in mission, equipping the troops to fight Jesus' holy war.

For centuries, pastors have been despised. They're considered effeminate, and many today are in fact female. I believe that God calls men, not women, to be pastors, and they have to be *men*, ready to act with courage, ready to fight, ready to lead. The Theopolitan vision aims to give you your marching orders.

But the Theopolitan vision isn't just for pastors. It's a vision for the *church*, and the church has vastly more non-pastors than pastors. The Spirit equips *every* man, woman, and child in the church with gifts to build the city and serve its mission.

More than the pastor, you non-pastor Theos and Theas straddle the boundary between the heavenly city and the earthly city. It's *you*, the people—the *laos*, "laity"—who take the word and bread and glory of worship out into the corners and byways of the cities of men. Filled with the Spirit, you are the agents of God's city who carry out Jesus' urban renewal program.

I should warn you at the beginning: The cities of men won't receive what you have to offer—not peaceably. Jesus warned His disciples that they would be beaten, arrested, scourged, crucified (Matt 10), and that is forever the life of the church. The world understands, sometimes better than Christians, how radical the gospel is, how fundamental the repentance it demands, how much things will have to change if the gospel is true. The world doesn't want to repent, and it doesn't like people who call for repentance.

Don't think for a moment that throwing yourself into the mission of God's city is a safe decision. Jesus calls you to lay down your life—perhaps in literal ways—to follow Jesus and build His city.

The world is always hostile to the church, but some worlds

are more hostile than others. Our world is more hostile than most, since it's built on an explicit rejection of Christian faith. Our world is also fracturing and decaying. Politically, geopolitically, economically, culturally, the world is crumbling. That only makes it more vicious: A cornered bear is a dangerous bear.

Tragically, many sectors of the church have become so worldly that they too are hostile to the demands of Jesus. If you call the church to repentance, be prepared for the assaults. Don't take up the task unless you're prepared to die.

Death isn't a defeat. Far from it. We share in Christ's dying so that we can share in His abundant life and glory. When we share in Christ's death, when we are like the early martyrs who did not "love life even to death" (Rev 12), we become a world-changing force. Courageous witness shatters old worlds and lays the foundations for new ones. It's through the cross that God's city renews the cities of men.

That is the Theopolitan vision of the city of God: a city founded on the blood of Jesus, sustained by the witness and blood of His disciples, established in the world to uproot and plant, to tear down and to build up.

1 BLESSED CITY

And he carried me away in Spirit to a great and high mountain
and showed me the holy city, Jerusalem,
coming down out of heaven from God.
Revelation 21:10

The book of Revelation has an odd ending. The third "in Spirit" vision (cf. Rev 1:9-10; 4:1-2) takes John into the wilderness, where he sees the harlot city Babylon drinking the blood of saints and riding on a scarlet beast (Rev 17:1-6). As he watches, the horns of the beast turn on Babylon, strip, eat, and burn her (17:16). Two chapters later, the beast and the false prophet—introduced as the sea and land beasts in chapter 13—are thrown into the lake of fire (19:19-21). Jesus chains Satan and sets the martyrs on thrones, where they reign for a thousand years (20:1-6).

After the thousand years, the dragon is released, deceives the nations, besieges the saints, but is consumed by fire from heaven and thrown into the lake of fire (20:7-10). A final judgment scene follows (20:11-15), and John sees the new heaven and new earth come from heaven, Jerusalem, the Bride who takes the place of the whore (21:1-8).

John has seen the church's three great enemies: the dragon (Rev 12), the sea and land beast (Rev 13) and the harlot (Rev 17). Then he sees them eliminated in reverse order: the harlot (Rev 17), the beasts (Rev 19), and the dragon (Rev 20). Finally the city descends, the city we look for, the future city whose builder and maker is God.

Everything's done. It's all neat and tidy. Time for the credits to roll. After all, what's left to see or say after a final judgment that ushers in a new heaven and new earth?

Here's the odd thing: There's *another* vision. One last time, John is caught up in Spirit, this time to a mountain (Rev 21:10). And—oddity on top of oddity—the vision is of "the holy city, Jerusalem, coming down out of heaven from God" (21:10). We'd excuse John if he tapped the angel on the shoulder and said, "Um. I've seen this one already."

What gives? Why does the city descend twice? Are there two cities?

No, there's only one city of God. To understand the final vision of Revelation, we have to remember the Old Testament. John isn't the first prophet to ascend a mountain and see a vision of a building. Moses climbed Sinai to see the "pattern" of the tabernacle (Exod 25:9, 40), the blueprints that guided Israel as they built God's house. Yahweh showed David the "pattern" of the temple and its furnishings (1 Chr 28:11-19), which he passed on to Solomon the temple builder. Ezekiel was shown a wondrous new temple, city, and land (Ezek 40–48), a set of plans to inspire the exiles returning from Babylon.

Prophets are sacred architects. The Spirit gives them plans, and then the same Spirit equips others to build according to the pattern.

That's what John is doing on the mountain at the end of Revelation: In Spirit, he sees the plan of heavenly Jerusalem and conveys the plans to his first readers and, centuries later, to us. And that same Spirit makes us wise craftsmen to build that city on earth. It's an ideal city, but it's an ideal that we are called to realize.

Revelation ends, in short, with an implied commission: "Go, build."

New Jerusalem is the people of God. We do long to enter the final city, but already *now* we're citizens of that city. The heavenly city is church in the *present*, not the final city of the future (which is described in Rev 21:1-8). It's you and me; it's us. It's us *right now*. It's the city where we already dwell, the city God wants us to keep building, repairing, beautifying until the end of all things.

That's the Theopolitan vision in a nutshell. The word "theo-polis" comes from two Greek words, *theos* and *polis*, and means "God's city." The Theopolitan vision is John's vision, a vision of the church, what the church is and does as a city among the nations.

Throughout this book, we'll be filling out the picture. I'll explain what this city does and what it looks like. We'll be coming back to Revelation 21 a lot. But for now, I want to do one simple thing: to convince you that the church is in fact a city among the cities of men.

Why do I need to convince you? Because many Christians are confused about the nature of the church.

What Is the Church?

Let's start with the obvious. When you say, "I'm a member of a church" or, "I'm going to church," what does the word "church" mean?

In the first instance, "church" doesn't refer to a building with a steeple. To see the church, you have to open the door to see all the people.

The church is *people*. Every Christian knows that. But it's so easy to forget. We need to follow through, doggedly, on that basic truth.

Because the church is people, it's a real-world community, as visible as any other group of people. Real people with real bodies and souls become members of the church through the rite of baptism, which uses water, the most abundant material substance on the planet. Real men and women and children with real bodies and souls gather regularly to hear a real man with a real tongue and vocal chords read and teach in real words from a book, to vibrate molecules of air with words of prayer and sung words of praise, to chew physical bread and drink physical wine at the Lord's table.

When we're not gathered, we (still real men and women and children with real bodies and souls) are supposed to pray for one another, encourage one another, help one another in times of crisis, weep and laugh and rant together. When we're not gathered, we strive to live lives faithful to Jesus, to take opportunities to be witnesses to Jesus, to cultivate faith in our families, to use our vocations to honor our Lord.

All of these are visible, bodily activities, photographable and video-able.

Local groups of Christians are often part of larger bodies. Anglicans are, in the main, part of the global Anglican Communion. Roman Catholics are part of a billion-plus-member church centered in Rome. Orthodox Christians are members of one or another family of Orthodox churches. Protestants group themselves into various denominations. First, Second, Third and up to Ninth Baptist Church may be all part of the Southern Baptist Convention, while First and Second and Third Presbyterian church come from different streams of Presbyterianism.

We can't see all the Anglicans or Catholics or Lutherans at once. But these wider networks consist of real men and women and children with real bodies and souls. These wider networks consist of local congregations that gather and disperse. They are as visible, as photographable and video-able in principle as the local gathering.

All of these different local communities and larger networks form the complex international reality of the "catholic" or universal church. This catholic church is as visible in principle as any sub-group within the catholic church. It would be theoretically possible, if practically unfeasible, to assemble all Christians from all over the world into one place (a corner of Texas would do), throw up a drone, and take a photo of the whole lot.

For all the specific differences among the subgroups, far-flung as we are, we're all recognizably part of the same real-world community. All these individuals and groups have certain things in common. What makes them all Christians is a common confession of Jesus Christ as Lord, many shared beliefs, a common baptism, a rhythm of liturgical gathering and missional dispersal.

Things are also somewhat more complicated. Some Christians wouldn't be able to show up for the group photo because they'd risk persecution if they openly professed Jesus.

There would be debates among those who show up about who belongs in the group photo and who doesn't. Some Catholics would want to keep their distance from anyone who is not in communion with Roman Pontiff. Some Protestants might want to take their own picture in another corner of Texas. Some Protestants would exclude Roman Catholics and Protestants outside their own denomination. Everyone would have to think about whether to make room for some of the odder African Independent Churches, whose links to historic Christianity are tenuous.

So there would be boundary disputes about who's in and who's out. But that doesn't make the church invisible. It means it's a visible global communion of local communities with fluid boundaries—just like every other real-world group, the Irish or Nigerians or the Masons.

The church is invisible because we can't see it all at once. The church is sometimes invisible because it has to go into hiding to survive. The church extends beyond the living to include the dead, from Adam and Abel on to yesterday's martyr. We commune with the whole church throughout all the ages, with saints who are visible and saints who are invisible. But those dimensions don't mean that "invisibility" is a defining quality of the church. The church's invisibility is empirical, not theological.

Think of Israel. Israel started with Abraham, a real man with a real body and a real wife named Sarah and (eventually) two sons and a company of servants. When Yahweh told Abraham to circumcise his household (Gen 17), he had only one son—Ishmael. The rest of the men and boys who got circumcised weren't related to Abraham by blood. They were part of his traveling city. This was the first Israel, marked out by the physical sign of circumcision, as visible as any nomadic company of men and women and children.

Throughout her history, Israel remained a visible community, a nation and a people. They escaped Egypt as a people, conquered the land as a people, established a monarchy as a people. Even when they were driven from the land, they retained their identity as a people, so that one day they could return to the land to rebuild the temple. Exile was the death of Israel as a visible people.

This *was* the people of God. What made them part of the same nation was their common trust in the God of the exodus, their common participation in the rites of worship, their common way of life.

Invisible Church?

Perhaps this surprises you. Perhaps someone taught you that "invisible" is a proper modifier for "church." Perhaps you learned that the *real* church is the invisible church.

The distinction between "visible" and "invisible" does capture some important truths. It's a way of saying that not everyone in the church will enjoy eternal life in the new creation and that some who are presently outside the church will one day join with the Bride. The visible/invisible distinction emphasizes that some churches, because of their disbelief and disobedience, negate the word and signs that define the church. There are invisible dimensions to the church—the Spirit's work that unites the members to Christ and to one another as His body.

The Bible says these things, but the Bible doesn't say them by talking about an invisible church. The Spirit's work is invisible, but the Spirit's work in itself isn't a "church." In the Bible, the church is a visible community among other communities of men and women and children—among nations, cities, families, social clubs, political parties, etc.

But you might say Paul tells us that "not all Israel is of Israel," that not everyone who was a member of the visible people of Israel was committed to the God of Israel. What makes someone a member of Israel in truth isn't circumcision but the condition of his heart.

That's a border dispute and doesn't change the fact that the true Israelite was a real man or woman or child with a real body, a member of a real historical people. There wasn't some invisible people of God lurking behind Israel. There wasn't a pristine history of faithfulness hidden in, with, or under the checkered history of Israel. The history of Israel—with all its triumphs and failures, its heroes and villains, its ups and downs—*that* is the history of the people of God.

But, you object: Sure, *Israel* was a visible community, but the church is an altogether different thing. Israel was defined by flesh, but there is no fleshly connection between members of the church. Israel was a visible physical people, but the church is an invisible spiritual community.

That's not the vision of the New Testament. Jesus was a real man with a real body, and He spent His earthly life gathering real men and women to be His disciples and to carry on as His little flock after His resurrection and ascension. Once they received the Spirit, they didn't cease being real men and women and children with real bodies and souls. Filled with the Spirit, they bore witness to Jesus, gathered to break bread and pray, testified to Jews and Gentiles, used the gifts of the Spirit to build up the community, called the body of Christ.

Christians get confused about this because they make a fundamental theological error. It's been a common theological error throughout the church's history, but that doesn't make it any less erroneous. That error is a "dualistic" understanding of nature and grace, or the natural and the supernatural.

That's a mouthful, so let me explain. The natural world includes Dalmatians and daisies, galaxies, quarks, and quasars. It also includes the natural activities that all human beings share in to one degree or another—eating and drinking and procreating, growing and preparing food. It includes social, economic, and cultural activities—labor, family and neighborhood organization, sculpture and sonatas, architecture and city planning, politics.

In a dualistic understanding, this natural and cultural world has its own laws and principles. Christians will confess that God created the natural world and providentially guides human history, of course. But the realm of nature doesn't belong to Christians. You don't need to be a Christian to know how to grow peas or write code. Christians don't have any monopoly of artistic skill;

it sometimes seems the opposite is true. The Bible doesn't tell you how to run your business or to win an election and lead a nation.

What Christianity offers—in this dualistic understanding—is communion with God, spiritual experience, forgiveness of sins, freedom from the curse. These blessings of salvation are *added* to the natural business of life. *In addition to* the insight I gain from observation, reason, science, I can gain spiritual insight from the Bible. That phrase "in addition to" is key: Christianity is a supernatural layer on top of the natural cake of life.

Dualism conceives of Christianity vertically: It sits on top of the natural world.

For a strict dualist, the "supernatural" doesn't touch natural life: The fact that I'm a Christian doesn't have *anything* to do with my work, business, family, politics. I read my Bible and listen to sermons to commune with Jesus, *not* to be told how to vote or spend my money. At its worst, this dualism can imply that Christianity is an escape from the demands of the natural world.

No Christian is a strict dualist in practice. It's hard to be a strict dualist if you've read any of the New Testament. Paul gives pretty explicit instructions about marriage and family (Eph 5–6), encourages us to work to the glory of God, and explains the purpose of civil government (Rom 13).

But many Christians are soft dualists when it comes to church. If you think of the church as an invisible, spiritual community, rather than a real-life visible society with and among other societies, you have a dualistic mindset. You're a dualist if you think that, in addition to the natural meals that keep your body chugging along, you now get to eat a supernatural meal at church, which keeps your soul chugging along. Church adds a supernatural dimension to my life but leaves my natural world more or less intact.

We should renounce nature-supernatural dualism and all its works and all its pomp. Everything comes from God. Creation is as much a gift of God's unmerited grace as redemption. Everything lives, moves, and has its being in God. Redemption transforms and fulfills nature; it's *not* a detached addition to it. Through His Spirit, Jesus is remaking and will remake everything about you and everything about the world.

Keep this in mind, because I'll come back to it several times during this book. For now, remember: The church isn't an invisible entity, a "supernatural" addition on top of natural human societies. The church is a transformed human society.

Instead of thinking vertically, we should think horizontally, which means thinking: The church is the future city that has entered into the present, the city we build that will be perfected in a new heavens and new earth.

People of the Triune God

I have emphasized—perhaps belabored—the visibility of the church, but I have good reason for it. Erroneous beliefs slip into our heads, and dangerous habits slip into our lives, when we don't acknowledge that the church is a real-world community of real men and women and children with real bodies and souls.

If we think the church is an invisible community of true believers, we might be tempted to avoid the mess of membership in a real community. After all, other people are tough to live with. If we pound a wedge between the "church-as-she-appears" and the "church-as-she-truly-is," we mistake the very nature of redemption. We might be tempted to think that being a Christian—being saved—means escaping from the real world with all its trials, temptations, and challenges, to search for a secret back door to God.

The Bible doesn't allow that option. There's only the front door, the west door, which is the entry door to the church. If you want to commune with your Creator, you're going to have to do it together with other real men and women and children with real bodies and souls, who also want to commune with their Creator. Redemption isn't escape from this world or from others. Redemption is becoming a member of a new society of which God's Spirit is the animating breath and of which Jesus Christ is head.

There's only the front door because the church—the visible, empirical communion of men and women and children—is *more than* a mere human society. It's a human society, but it's an utterly unique human society. *As* a visible society, with its fluid boundaries, for all its checkered history, the church *is* the people of the Triune God. It is a communion of real-life human beings joined in communion with the Creator.

The New Testament describes the church in relation to each person of the Trinity.

- We are adopted children of our heavenly Father (1 John 3:1), and thus constitute a family of brothers and sisters (Matt 12:48-50). The family of the Father isn't some inaccessible invisible family but the real-world church. If you want to be a child of God, you have to be among the children of God.
- We are the body of Christ, each of us a member and organ of Christ as our eyes, ears, hands, and feet are members of our personal body (Rom 12; 1 Cor 12; Eph 4). If you want to be united to Christ, you need to be united to His body.
- As the body of Christ, the church is animated by the Spirit of Jesus. The Spirit distributes gifts to each part (1 Cor 12), enables the body to build itself up into maturity (Eph 4), sanctifies us as saints. The Spirit prays in and through our groans (Rom 8). The church is the temple of that Spirit (1 Cor 3:16). You can't be a living stone in that Spiritual temple unless you're part of a structure made of living stones.

All of these descriptions of the church—children of the Father, body of the incarnate Son, temple of the Spirit—are descriptions of the real-world, historical community of real men and women and children with real bodies and souls. They're all descriptions of the heavenly city that has taken its place among the cities and nations of men.

In His "high priestly" prayer (John 17), Jesus prays that the disciples would be one as He is one with the Father. That unity is a unity of mutual indwelling: The Son is in the Father, and the Father is in the Son. Jesus prays that His disciples would form a communion so deeply one that it resembles this divine unity of mutual indwelling.

Jesus also prays that the disciples would be incorporated into the mutual indwelling of the Father and Son: "they in Us . . . I in them and Thou in Me" (vv. 21, 23). Just as the Father indwells the Son who indwells Him, so the disciples of Jesus are indwelt by the God whom they also simultaneously indwell. God makes the disciples His home, even as He is the disciples' home. Jesus wants His disciples to become part of the "society" that exists between the Father and Son in the Spirit.

This communion of mutual indwelling among disciples—this *church*—is a *visible* communion of disciples. Jesus doesn't bring His disciples to communion with God by elevating up and out of their bodies to swirl in invisible spiritual bliss. The disciples don't form a communion that is visible only to the "eyes of faith." It's a communion visible to the *world*, with a unity visible to the world (17:21). The church's unity of mutual indwelling should be visible enough to convince the unbelieving *world* that the Father sent the Son.

The church has invisible dimensions and depths, deep as the depths of God Himself. But these invisible dimensions are depths of a real-world church. *As* a real-world people, made of up real men and women and children with real bodies and souls, the visible church is called to manifest on earth the eternal communion of Father and Son.

That means you and your fellow church members, in whatever kind of church you are and wherever you live. Together with your brothers and sisters, you are a visible people joined with one another because the Spirit has brought you into communion with the Father and Son. Your home church is a family of the Father, united as the body of the incarnate Son, indwelt by the Spirit. Your mundane, apparently pathetic little church is the greatest mystery in the universe.

God's Future Polis

You've followed this far. You may be skeptical, suspicious, even angry—at me or at someone who misled you in the past. If you've come this far, I'm going to risk another step: The church isn't simply a real-world, visible and historical society of real-life men, women, and children with real bodies and souls. It's a particular *kind* of human society.

The church is a *city*. It's the heavenly city, the city of the *future*.

This brings up another invisible dimension of the church, another reason to say that the church isn't just another interest group, club, or nation. Remember the beginning of this chapter: John sees the heavenly city descend *twice*. The first descent comes *after* the final judgment. It's the final city, the new heavens and the new earth. The second vision of the city shows the city in history and provides the pattern that guides our building in the present.

The city of God is the present form of a future city. It's the city that will one day be identical with the new heavens and new earth. Rome rose and fell. London was once the center of an empire but has contracted. Washington's dominance of the world won't last forever, nor will Beijing's (if China's the next lord of history).

But the city of God *will* last until the end and beyond the end. The church is the present presence of a perfect city to come. It's the *now* of a city that is not yet. Your mundane, apparently pathetic home church is a people in communion with the Triune God. It's also an outpost of a perfect new creation, future utopia here and now, ahead of time. You should greet one another as if you were in a SciFi movie: "Hi, I'm from the future. Are you?"

Because the church is the presence of God's city, His theopolis, the church is inherently *political*. It's inherently like a city, a civic reality. The New Testament makes this clear in the terminology it uses to describe the church, nearly all of which comes from ancient political theory.

Outside the New Testament, the term "church" (Gr. *ekklesia*) refers to an assembly, a calling-together, of the citizens of an ancient Greek city-state. Faced with military threat, political upheaval, or natural disaster, citizens gathered as the *ekklesia* to deliberate about what to do. The good order and future of the city depended on the work of the assembly.

For the early Christians, the church is God's assembly, with its own civic order, its own leaders, its own festivals and rituals, its own way of life. And the early Christians believed their assemblies—their *ekklesiai*—determined the future of the city where they assembled. The flourishing and future of Ephesus didn't depend on the *ekklesia* of Ephesian citizens. It depended on the assembly of Ephesian saints who called on the name of the Lord. No matter how small or weak by the world's standards, the Christian *ekklesiai*, because they were the body of Christ the Lord of all, had their hands on the reins of history.

John describes the church as a *koinonia* (1 John 1:7), a participation in the common good of the Spirit, using a term that Aristotle used to describe the "community" of the city. Ancient thinkers imagined nations as political "bodies," like the body of Christ (Rom 12; 1 Cor 12). Paul tells the Philippians that their "citizenship" is in heaven (Phil 3:20-21). Peter draws from Exodus 19 to describe the church as a holy *nation* (1 Pet 2:9-10).

The formation of God's *polis* is inherent in the gospel. Jesus didn't die and rise again simply to rescue us from the eternal torments of hell. He *did* that, but that was not the limit of His work. He died in order to break down the dividing wall between Jew and Gentile and form a new human race, constituted from men and women from every tribe, tongue, people, and nation (Eph 2:11-22). He is the new Abel, who suffered outside the gates, not to found a Cainite Babel but to found new Jerusalem.

The good news is that Jesus has dealt with our sin and given us new life in the Spirit. The good news is *equally* that Jesus has founded a new city on the earth, a city as visible as any other city, full of real-life men and women and children with real bodies and souls, a city with a real history. The gospel calls us to repent and seek the mercy of Christ. It also calls us to leave the world behind to become members of a new society, the body of Christ. The gospel is fundamentally political; the church, God's *polis*, is embedded within it.

Human beings are social creatures. God created us to speak to, work with, love one another. It was not good for Adam to be alone, and so God provided a helper suitable to him. Together they formed a "we," a family. It's not good for families to be alone, so human beings form larger groupings, the larger "we" of a tribe, city, or nation.

If God is to save human beings as we actually are—social and civic creatures—then He has to save us in our social and civic relationships and institutions. If God has acted in history to save the world—if salvation is a reality *now*—then it *must* take the form of a redeemed community, a redeemed city.

The church isn't merely a means for individuals to be saved. The church isn't a channel of salvation. The church is humanity saved. The church *is* communion with God and one another in God; it is the future perfect city in an imperfect present. The church *is* salvation in social form.

City on a Mission

Salvation is an eschatological reality from top to bottom. Jesus proclaims that the kingdom of God is near. He says that His death is the judgment of this world and the casting out of the prince of this world (John 12). When He dies, He announces, "It is finished." By His resurrection and ascension, Jesus enters fully into the new creation, the Last Adam who has become life-giving Spirit (1 Cor 15).

We're united to Christ by the Spirit and thus receive a share in the new creation. Paul says that wherever anyone is in Christ, new creation has broken through into the old (2 Cor 5:17). We're united to the risen Christ *together* so that the church, filled with the Spirit, *is* new creation. This message is inherent in the gospel: The future has taken root in the present, the coming kingdom *has* come, the new Jerusalem has nestled among the nations.

For the present, and until Jesus returns, the city of God remains flawed. Her blemishes are all-too-obvious. Her history will continue to bump up and down. There will be villains as well as heroes. But the church—the real-world visible church, the historical communion of real men and women and children with real bodies and souls—*that* church is the present form of the future city. She is presently the bride who will be unveiled in glory at the last judgment.

We still look for a city whose builder and maker is God. We hope for a bridal city to unite heaven and earth forever. But we also believe that this city already has an earthly address. The world is dotted with outposts of the heavenly city. It is a sign of a future city, but not a "mere sign." It's an *effective* sign, a present sign that gives us a taste now of the city to come.

The church's mission is, in the first instance, simply to *be* what the Lord says she is: the family of the Father, the body of Christ, the temple of the Spirit. The church's vocation is to be a communion of disciples, each dwelling in each as they dwell together in the God who dwells in them. The church's vocation is to proclaim the gospel, teach the commandments of Jesus, baptize converts and their children, break bread, encourage and correct.

John has brought the blueprints from the mountain. For two millennia, Christians have been building. We're called to do our share in that cosmic construction project.

The heavenly city isn't static. It's not merely *placed* in the world, among the cities and nations of men. God established His city among the cities of men to *redeem* those human cities. Jesus commissioned the church to disciple nations. He established His city to engage in an urban renewal project.

In cities full of dislocated and disoriented strangers, the church offers communion and the safety of home. In food deserts, the church gives bread. Where men are enslaved to addictive sin, the church proclaims the good news of liberation through the Spirit who breaks chains and raises the dead. To addicts and prostitutes who hide themselves in shame, the church preaches the blood of Jesus that cleanses sin and the gift of the Spirit who clothes in glory. When politicians prey on the weak, the church steps in to defend the vulnerable and demand justice. In cities of greed and gluttony, the church proclaims the fruits of the Spirit. Where housing collapses, the church opens a homeless shelter.

The church's mission isn't hopeless. The hope the church offers isn't merely a hope for the distant future, a future after death. God has announced His kingdom and established His city to fulfill His promise to Abraham, the promise to bless the nations. The kingdom came as a stone that shattered the empires of the ancient world. But it's God's kingdom, the fifth monarchy, that will grow into a mountain that fills the whole earth (Dan 2). The Son of Man inherits the dominion of the bestial ancient empires so that the saints of the highest one reign in the authority given by the Ancient of Days (Dan 7).

The city of God is a city of light that illumines a dark world (Rev 21:23-24). It's the source of living waters, which brings life to a desert land (22:1-5). Through the Son and Spirit, the Lord has established Zion as the chief of the mountains, Jerusalem as the queen of cities. As the law of Yahweh flows out, the nations are drawn to Zion to learn the Lord's ways. They beat their swords into ploughs and their spears into pruning hooks, transforming weapons of war into tools of peaceful productivity (Isa 2:1-4). Jesus has been raised and enthroned, and He *will* reign until all His enemies, including death itself, are placed beneath His feet.

That is to say, the church *will* fulfill the mission that Jesus has assigned her. The city of God, sent to renew the cities of men, *will* renew the cities of men.

Over the centuries, millions upon millions of individuals will hear the gospel, be awakened by the Spirit, be baptized into the body of Christ, and live in Christian faithfulness. But the church's mission doesn't end with the gathering of a global network of local churches. As she gathers individuals, the church disrupts the patterns of corporate life in the cities of men, dismantles institutions of injustice and structures that promote ungodliness. As the church is the church, as she is the people of the Triune God, as she is the effective sign of the city to come, Jesus' Spirit transforms families, tribes, cities, nations through the ministries of the church.

The church that carries out this mission is the church of Jesus Christ, the crucified and risen Lord. *Crucified* Lord. Jesus didn't go to the cross to save us the trouble of sharing the cross. The opposite is true: Jesus went to the cross to give us a share in His suffering so that, in Him, we can offer ourselves for the life of the world.

The city of man is quite content to be what it has always been. It doesn't like to be disrupted, and the church is a disruption. The church's very existence is a rebuke to the city of man, to the world's pretensions, idolatries, violence, lusts, perversions. The rebuke stings, and the city of man responds violently to the sting.

We will complete the mission Jesus has given us, but we'll complete that mission in the way Jesus did: by suffering, by enduring hatred and unreasonable opposition, through brutal attacks from the world and sometimes from other citizens of the city of God. That opposition doesn't spell defeat. It's the way of victory. When we suffer in Christ, we dynamite the foundations of the city so that a new city can be built from the rubble.

Some cities are friendlier to the church. Some cities and nations profess Christ. That's not a problem. That's the aim of Christian mission, that all nations would acknowledge the Lord as King. Yet the church can *never* be complacent. We are still called to bear the cross. If the church never provokes the city of man, we're probably not being faithful to the crucified Lord of the church, who has called us to take up the cross to follow Him.

The Theopolitan Alternative

Christians today feel that the world is coming apart at the seams. Politically, economically, culturally, morally, everything seems to be in upheaval. Christians have responded by proposing various remedies: political strategies, tactical withdrawals into quasi-monastic communities of virtue, compromise.

Most of these responses miss the heart of the matter.

Central to the Theopolitan vision is the conviction that the church drives history, for good or ill. Political and cultural trends are secondary to happenings and movements in the church.

The needs of the world can only be met by the Triune God, and He has caught the church up in his work of renewing and glorifying creation. The cities of men can be revived and renewed only as the Spirit of Jesus works through the real-world communion of real men and women and children with real bodies and souls that constitutes the church. The cities of men can be renewed only by that community that shares the suffering and glory of Jesus through his Spirit.

When the world is in disarray, we hope for another world. We want to grasp utopia. But utopia is in our midst. The other world—the world of the future—has become present through Jesus and His Spirit, as the church of Jesus Christ. Only the church can bring the powers of the age to come into the present age. Because it is the Spirit-filled Bride and Body of the Son of God, only the city of God gives hope to the cities of men.

2   TASTING THE END

And the city is laid out as a square,
and its length is as great as the width. . . .
its length and width and height are equal.
Revelation 21:16

The Theopolitan vision is a vision of the church in her relation to the world. It highlights the political nature and mission
of the church and the political character of the gospel that the
church proclaims. Jesus founded the city of God among the cities
of men to witness and to transform those cities. God will fulfill
the commission Jesus gave the church. The nations are being,
and will continue to be, discipled. The kingdoms of this world
have become and are becoming the kingdom of our Lord and of
His Christ.

How does that happen? Is this anything more than wishful-
ness or nostalgia?

It happens because the church is a city whose length, breadth,
and height are the same.

Say what? What do the dimensions of new Jerusalem have to
do with the mission of the church? Much in every way.

From a mountain, John, like Moses, sees the pattern of heaven. He writes it and sends it to the church so that we can replicate the heavenly pattern on earth. He gives us the blueprints. We're the builders.

Nearly every phrase and clause of John's description of new Jerusalem comes from an Old Testament text. The city has twelve gates, marked with the names of the tribes of Israel, three gates at each point of the compass (Rev 21:12-13). It's a civilized (i.e., "citified") version of Israel's wilderness camp, when three tribes camped on each of the four sides of the tabernacle.

The city gleams like a jewel, like pure gold (Rev 21:11, 18). Her foundation stones are gemstones, twelve of them (21:19-20). With her gold walls and streets, she resembles the temple with its gold-plated walls and floor. Her twelve gemstones are like the gems on the breastplate of the high priest (Exod 28). Jerusalem is a bridal city, but she's dressed like a priest. The throne of God and of the Lamb is in the city, the source of living water (22:1).

These descriptions aren't grabbed randomly from a thesaurus of biblical imagery. They form a coherent overall picture: The city is Israel, the camp of Israel, the temple, a priestly city.

The dimensions reinforce this in a particular way. The city is a cube, like the Most Holy Place of Israel's tabernacle and temple (Exod 26:31-33; 1 Kgs 6:20). Jerusalem is the inner sanctuary all growed up into a city.

Let's take a moment to pause over that. The Most Holy Place was Yahweh's throne room, inaccessible to any but the high priest (Lev 16:1-2). In new Jerusalem, the citizens *live* in the throne room, serving the Lord and seeing His face (Rev 22:3-4). The Most Holy Place was the center of Israel's liturgical system. The temple occupied a large portion of ancient Jerusalem, but there was a difference between temple and city. In new Jerusalem, though, the gap between city and temple has been closed. The equal dimensions tell us that the *whole* city is liturgical space, of the holiest variety.

That gives us a clue about the work of the city of God among the cities of men. The church is the Spirit's instrument for accomplishing God's mission, and the church's participation in mission centers what happens in the sanctuary. We carry out our mission through the proclamation and teaching of the word of God, liturgical gathering around the Lord's word and table, faithful witness to the kingship of Jesus, and careful pastoral guidance.

As the church does her churchy things, she brings the life of the age to come to the nations. We're builders of the city, and the chief labor of building takes place on our day of rest, in the liturgy. We all are builders because the liturgy is the work of the whole people, not merely the work of the pastor. The church fulfills Jesus' mission by being what she is, a *liturgical* city.

Mission starts with liturgy. Liturgy is the time and place where the church gathers as the city council, the *ekklesia* of God, an assembly of the heavenly city. As the real men and women and children with real bodies and souls gather for worship and disperse from worship, heavenly life comes to earth. Having tasted the good things of the age to come, the church goes out to share those goods in the marketplace. The sanctuary, the place of worship and communion with God, is the center of the world. It always has been, right from the beginning.

Or, put it this way:

Watch the Water

When God first created the world, He mapped it into several territories. He planted a garden in the east of a land called Eden. Outside Eden were other lands, like the land of Havilah where the Creator buried gold and precious stones. The world wasn't homogenous but differentiated. From the beginning, God organized the world into a garden, a land, and a wider world.

Eden's garden was the original sanctuary, the place of

worship and communion with God (Gen 2). At the center of the garden were two trees, a tree that communicated life and a tree that opened eyes to give knowledge of good and evil. Yahweh intended to commune with Adam and Eve in the garden. When He expelled them, He set up cherubim at the gate to keep them out. Later sanctuaries are full of cherubim figures (Exod 25:18-22; 1 Kgs 6:23-28), guardians of the house and throne room of Yahweh.

Adam and Eve had other responsibilities in the other zones of creation. They were commissioned to fill, subdue, and rule the earth. They would trek down to Havilah to mine the gold and precious stones. The garden was planted within the land of Eden, a land that would serve as humanity's first home. Adam and Eve were called to work in the land and to have dominion in the world. In the garden, they were called to worship.

A river sprang up in the land of Eden and flowed through the garden (Gen 2). From there, it split into four rivers that went out to the corners of earth. Water sprang up from the higher ground of the land, where the Lord was enthroned, but flowed through the sanctuary before it spread to the world. Living water from the presence of God was mediated to the world through the place of worship.

Throughout the Bible, sanctuaries are "well-watered places," like the garden of God. In the courtyard of the tabernacle was a laver full of water for cleansing sacrifices and priests (Exod 30:17-21). In Solomon's temple, that laver had expanded into a gigantic bronze sea, carried on the backs of twelve oxen (1 Kgs 7:23-26). The bronze sea depicted the vocation of Israel among the nations. As a cosmic image, it showed that Israel was the "Atlas" nation, bearing the firmament on it shoulders, holding up the heavenly waters above. As an image of international order, it showed that Israel bore the "sea of nations" on their backs. The temple in Jerusalem, not Babylon or Susa or Athens or Rome, was the axis of the ancient world.

Solomon made ten water basins on wheeled structures that resembled chariots (1 Kgs 7:27-37). Heavenly water was available in the house of God, but the chariots hinted that the Lord was sending water out to the world. Solomon's temple had a reservoir, but it was also the source of a river—just like Eden.

After describing the new temple in excruciating detail, Ezekiel spies water flowing from the house (Ezek 47). At first, it's only a little trickle from the throne of God, streaming out into the temple courts. As it crosses the temple threshold, it gets wider and deeper and keeps growing as it flows down from Zion out to the land. First, the water is up to Ezekiel's ankles, then to his knees, and finally so deep he cannot cross it. As it flows, *where* it flows, trees spring up, bearing fruit. Ezekiel's river flows east, all the way to the Dead Sea, where it freshens the salt water and brings dead fish to life. It's a vision of God's transforming work in the world, but the source of the water is crucial to the vision: It brings life as it flows from the sanctuary, out of the place of worship.

In the recesses of the Most Holy Place, Yahweh kept His treasure chest under His cherubim throne. That chest—known as the ark of the covenant—contained three things: the tablets of the law from Sinai, a jar of manna from the wilderness, and Aaron's rod that budded and bore fruit in the presence of the Lord (Heb 9:4). No ancient Israelite was permitted to enter the Most Holy Place to enjoy these treasures. In Ezekiel, that changes. The river that flows from Ezekiel's temple begins from that very throne room. It carries Yahweh's hidden treasures out to the world.

Ezekiel's river is a picture of Israel. The people gather to receive the word of the Lord from the priests and to feast in His presence. When they disperse, they are themselves the living waters, flowing out to the nations.

As we've seen, the Bible ends with a similar vision. John sees the new Jerusalem descend as a Bride from heaven.

Nations stream into her, bringing their treasures. And a river flows through her, lined with trees of life that bear fruit every month and whose leaves bring healing to the nations (Rev 22:1-5). It's a vision of the church as sanctuary, a place of worship that serves as the source of life-giving water to the nations. It's a vision of the church as a community whose liturgical life is for the life of the world.

Revelation also provides a contrary example. When the third trumpet sounds, a star falls onto the springs and rivers (Rev 8:10-11). The star is named Wormwood, and it poisons the water sources, which turns the water deadly. Springs and rivers represent the temple in Jerusalem as the source of life, but the temple has become so corrupt that she spreads death rather than life.

The church's liturgy is a source of life or death to the world. It's a spring of living water or a fountain of poison. How can we tell whether the church's worship is spreading life or death? What kind of worship is a source of life-giving water to the world?

At one level, the answer is simple: The church's worship brings life if it conforms to God's requirements for worship. It brings life if it's shaped and saturated by God's word. What might that mean?

Biblical Worship

The church's worship is a source of life when it is conformed to the word of God. The first commandment demands exclusive worship of Yahweh, but the Lord isn't satisfied with telling us *whom* to worship. He also tells us *how* to worship. God gave liturgical instructions to Israel, which are far more detailed than the instructions He gave them about, say, private property or environmental justice. And the rules that governed the sanctuary carried stiff penalties. Nadab and Abihu offered "strange fire" and received fire in return, burn for burn (Lev 10).

Christian worship is different from the worship of ancient Israel, *radically* so. At Jesus' death, the veil of the temple was torn from top to bottom, a sign that there would be free comings and goings into the house of God. The church as a whole is not most sacred space. We now gather before the Lord unveiled, without a screen to separate the people from the presence of the Lord or the Lord from the people. Jesus the heavenly High Priest has entered the heavenly sanctuary, and by His Spirit He brings out the hidden treasures of heaven—the heavenly word and the bread of angels.

Christian worship is radically different from the worship of ancient Israel, but it is no less governed by the word. Christian worship, like the worship of Israel, must be worship by the book. It must be biblical.

When you hear that, you might immediately think of the depictions of early Christian worship in Acts or 1 Corinthians. You might think that Christian worship must be guided by *New Testament* teaching about worship.

Christians live in a new covenantal order, but it's a dangerous error to think that the New Testament *alone* is our guide for worship or for anything.

We can't even know what worship is unless we understand Leviticus, *the* biblical book about worship. And we can't grasp Leviticus without knowing Eden and the exodus. We can't grasp the biblical teaching about liturgical music without immersing ourselves in the Psalms and 1-2 Chronicles. We won't understand the meaning of holy communion unless we glimpse the rich biblical theology of food and festivity, which runs from Genesis 1 to Revelation 22. When we say Christian worship must be biblical, we mean it must be patterned by the *whole* Bible.

Later volumes in this series will spell out details of liturgical theology and practice in more depth, but let me offer some illustrations of how the whole Bible helps us answer liturgical questions.

- *Is there a right order of worship?*
  In Scripture, worship is covenant renewal, and covenant ceremonies are arranged in a specific sequence of actions. Israel gathers at Sinai, purifies herself for the Lord's appearance, hears the word, and then feasts in the Lord's presence (Exod 19—24). When Israelites offered a series of sacrifices, they began with a sin offering for cleansing, added an ascension offering to enter the presence of God, and ended with a peace offering that involved a meal (Num 6; 2 Chr 29:20-33). Israel's order of worship anticipates the order of historic Christian liturgies: confession and cleansing; consecration in word; communion at the Lord's table. Historic liturgies often divide the service into a liturgy of the word (*synaxis*) and a liturgy of the table (Eucharist). That's an error. Biblically, the liturgy is a united sequence of actions, a single complex act of covenant renewal.
- *What posture should we adopt at the Lord's table?*
  There is no biblical command, but various considerations indicate that we should sit for communion. Jesus commanded the multitudes sit before He fed them (Matt 14:19; Mark 6:39; John 6:10). Sitting is the posture of kings, and the Lord's table is a table for the king's friends (John 15:13-14; cf. 1 Kgs 4:5). The Supper is celebration, not contrition; we eat and drink as priest-kings, not as penitents.
- *Should the church observe a church calendar?*
  There's no command to observe a church calendar, but Israel's worship provides a guide (Lev 23; Deut 14—16). Each year, Israel commemorated the great acts of Yahweh in the exodus (Passover), the giving of the law (Pentecost), and the preservation of Israel in the wilderness (Feast of Booths). Israel's weeks were structured by a dance of work and Sabbath, and her year also had a liturgical rhythm. The church does well to follow Israel's example in this regard.

- *Should a minister wear a robe when he leads the liturgy?*
  There is no command for pastors to wear robes, but Israel again provides a salutary example. The priests wore distinctive clothing that manifested their office (Exod 28). Throughout Scripture, clothing is a mark of authority and glory (cf. Gen 37:37-45; 1 Sam 15:27; 1 Kgs 11:26-40). The church isn't a democracy. There are leaders and rulers in the church, as there are in any city. Liturgical roles aren't interchangeable. The hierarchical character of church order should be manifested in the liturgy.
- *Should there be any artwork in the place of worship?*
  Israel's sanctuaries were richly adorned with gold, embroidered images of cherubim and plants, carvings of palm trees and flowers (Exod 25–31; 1 Kgs 6–8). The decorations signified that the sanctuaries are reconstituted Edens. The second commandment didn't prohibit making images or even placing images in the sanctuary. It prohibited using images as a means for making contact with God (Exod 20:4-6). It still does. Scripture rejects icon veneration in the strongest terms.

To say that worship must be biblical doesn't only mean that Scripture teaches us what we do and don't do in worship or that Scripture teaches us what worship is and means. Worship must be biblical also in the sense that it *includes* Bible reading and Bible teaching. God spoke to Israel from Sinai in a context of covenant-making, a liturgical setting. The early Christians gathered to pray and break bread, also to receive the apostles' teaching. Christian liturgy is a liturgy of *word* and table.

A Christian worship service that minimizes the place of Scripture isn't too liturgical. It's not liturgical enough.

The church's liturgy should be Bible-saturated. There should be readings from Scripture, generous readings, not a few snippets from a lectionary or a few lines as a sermon text. The readings shouldn't skip the difficult or embarrassing parts— the tent pegs through the brains, the details about the impurity of menstruation, the severe things Jesus and Paul have to say about first-century Jews.

In worship, the congregation should *listen* to the word read, receiving it by ear. We can read with our eyes at home. We should *sing* the Scriptures in Psalms and *speak* the Scriptures to one another in liturgical dialogue—rolling the word on our tongues. The pastor should teach the Bible—the *Bible*, not a review of the week's news or an anecdote from his personal life. The sermon isn't an occasion for a theological lecture. But it should be substantial, as solid as the congregation can handle. Pastors should aspire to offer solid food rather than skim milk, oatmeal stout rather than Bud Light.

The liturgy is the primary location for the church's encounter with Scripture. The liturgy does more than communicate things *about* the Bible. In the liturgy, we are brought into the story of the Bible and begin to inhabit the world the Bible describes. Through the word in the liturgy, our lives are taken up into the great narrative of redemption. They become subplots of the story of the world, the story that is reenacted each week.

Let's make this concrete: Within the liturgy, the hundreds of biblical stories about food become *our* story as we share the Lord's table. God feeds *us* too, as He fed Adam, Abraham, Israel, David, the multitudes who followed Jesus. The dozens of water crossings and water rescues are realized in the church in baptism. In the liturgy, we commune with the living God, standing in the place of Adam, Abraham, Moses, Aaron, Israel, David, Jeremiah, Isaiah, and all the rest. Their stories and experiences become ours—not in pretense but in reality.

Through the word in worship, we become more than a people with Bible knowledge. We become a people molded inside and out, in our imaginations and identity, in our minds and hearts, by Scripture. The Bible presses its patterns on us. It seeps into us so that we become a Bible-shaped people whose veins bleed bibline.

Festive worship

Christian worship is word-centered worship. As real men and women and children with real bodies and souls gather, we hear the word read and taught, sing the word, speak the word. And, crucially, we *eat* the word.

The Lord's Supper should be part of *every* Lord's day liturgy. Worship in the Bible *always* takes place at a table. An altar is a table (cf. Ezek 41:22), and ever since the flood, the people of God have erected altars at places of worship (Gen 8:20; 12:7-8; 33:20; Exod 20:24).

If you could see an ancient Israelite preparing for a feast, you'd see him pick an unblemished animal from his flock or herd, prepare flour or bread, and grab a flagon of wine. If you didn't know better, you might suspect he's preparing for a barbeque. Because he *is*. At the tabernacle and temple, priests offer the Lord's bread, and worshipers share His food (cf. Lev 21—22). Covenant renewal climaxes with a covenant meal, a sign of restored harmony between the parties to the covenant.

Biblically, worship without a meal isn't worship at all. When we worship without the Supper, it's as if we're disciples on the road to Emmaus, who hear Jesus speak but never recognize Him because we don't stick around for the breaking of bread (Luke 24). A liturgy without the Supper is like a contract without signatures; it *is* (not just *like*) a wedding feast without food, a party without hors d'oeuvres and wine, as if the Lord were to open His house to extend hospitality but never offer chips or bring the beer out of the fridge.

Neglect and abuse of the Lord's Supper is one of the disasters of church history. In the medieval church, "lay" Christians were all but excluded from the meal, which had been re-defined and reserved for the priests. The Reformers demanded bread for ordinary Christians. All the baptized are priests, Luther insisted, by virtue of their baptism; all are holy, and the Supper is holy food for the holy ones. Calvin wanted to have the Supper every week.

After that sound start, much of the Protestant world drifted into the old medieval neglect of the Supper. Of course, Protestants *say* they're doing the opposite. They say they have the Supper infrequently to keep it special. That doesn't fly. Protestants are supposed to follow the Bible in liturgy and life, but with regard to the Supper, many have adopted a position that is *completely* at odds with biblical conceptions of worship.

Restoring the Supper to its central place in Christian worship should be one of the church's highest priorities. Without it, we cannot be the source of living water to the world. Without it, we will not be effective as the heavenly city on a mission to transform the cities of men.

Does this sound extreme? To some Protestant ears, this sounds like a demand to reverse the Reformation and return to Rome. It sounds like a call to give up the word-centeredness of worship for dead sacramentalism. You might be thinking, "Who would want to have the Lord's Supper every week anyway? It's dreary and depressing, all that self-examination and anxiety, all that gloom and contrition. It leaves me depressed." Or, you might be thinking, "It extends worship by a good half hour, and I need to get home for the kickoff."

These objections rest on a superficial understanding of the Supper. Let me start with the final more "practical" objections. It's true that many churches, including many Protestant churches, celebrate the Lord's Supper as if it were a wake. (That's not quite right. Wakes can be raucous affairs. But you get the idea.) Many churches keep the Lord's Supper as if they were gathering at a tomb rather than a table; and that tomb isn't an empty one. Paul's exhortation to self-examination becomes the dominant motif to the whole event (1 Cor 11).

We should take Paul with utter seriousness. We must come

to the table worthily, and that means we have to engage in self-examination and repentance. But that self-examination doesn't take place *at* the table. The table is, well, a *table*. Bread is food, and wine is a festive drink. *Nowhere* in the Bible do people gather at a table to mourn their sins. If God wanted us to mourn our sins, He would have commanded a weekly fast, not a weekly feast.

Tables are for eating, drinking, and rejoicing. In Israel, the sanctuary was a place of joy, where Israel could eat, drink, and rejoice (Deut 12). When Israel gathered, they were to eat, drink, and rejoice (Deut 16). If we celebrate the Lord's Supper as it *ought* to be celebrated, every Lord's Day will be a day of gladness, and every worship service will be a journey into joy.

The Supper commemorates the gruesome death of Jesus on the cross. "Commemorate" is too weak. It's not merely that we remember the death of Jesus. We eat and drink the death of Jesus so that, like our daily food, His sacrifice becomes part of us, so that our flesh is conformed to His flesh, and our veins flow with His blood. To share in the Lord's Supper is to share in the sacrifice of Jesus and so to be called to a life of continuous sacrifice.

As I stressed in chapter 1, we cannot hope for painless renewal in the church or the world. The church is renewed by sharing by the Spirit in the dying and rising of Jesus. The church is made a new body through a painful passage of dismemberment. The world must be shattered to pieces before it can be rebuilt. Every time we receive the body and blood of Jesus, we're called to become, and we *are* becoming, a community of sacrifice, a people prepared for world-destroying, world-building witness.

Yet I have said that the Supper is an overflowing cup not an empty plate, bright laughter not black morbidity. How can we rejoice when we share the cup of Jesus that calls us to a life of self-emptying love?

We rejoice in the cup of sacrifice because we follow Jesus. He suffered agony in Gethsemane, but He went to the cross for the joy that was set before Him (Heb 12:2), the joy of His vindication and glorification. That joyful fulfillment is in our past, and in the Supper we rejoice *now* in the joy that is yet to come. We taste heavenly joy so that we can, like Jesus, take up the cross in gladness. Or: We recognize the privilege of suffering with Jesus so that the meal of joy and the meal of self-sacrifice are one meal. Like the disciples, we rejoice that we are worthy to suffer shame for His name (Acts 5:41).

Regular celebration of the Supper keeps the church Christ-centered. Preachers preach on all sorts of things, quite properly so, because the Bible addresses all and everything. But all things cohere in Christ (Col 1:17). Whatever the sermon topic, the incarnation, death, resurrection, ascension and reign of the Son of God is at the heart of the sermon. The Supper keeps the preacher on point, forcing him to connect every topic or text to the central reality of Jesus.

A preacher may preach on the case laws of Exodus or the genealogies of 1 Chronicles, but then he has to stand at the table. Even if he doesn't say anything to connect the sermon to the Supper, the connection is made: The case laws somehow reveal Christ; the genealogies are part of the back-story of Jesus.

During Jesus' conversation with the disciples on the road to Emmaus, He tells them *"everything* concerning Himself in all the Scripture"* (Luke 24). The whole Bible is about Jesus. But Jesus has a body, and so everything in the Bible that is about Jesus—which is *everything*—is also about His body, the church. And this Jesus, who is the center of Scripture and who has a churchly body, also offers His body and blood to us in bread and wine. Thus: everything in the Bible that is about Jesus—which is *everything*—also discloses some facet of the Eucharistic meal.

Jesus is the new Adam, and in Him we are a new Adamic humanity, admitted to the garden to eat from the trees of life and knowledge (Gen 2). Jesus is the seed of Abraham, and in Him we gather for a meal with the Triune God (Gen 18). Jesus tabernacles among us (John 1:14); His body is the temple (John 2:21), and so we gather to Him to eat, drink, and rejoice in His presence. Jesus is the new Moses, leading us out of Egypt and giving Himself as true bread from heaven. Jesus is the Bridegroom, and the Supper is a love feast where the Bride feasts on the body of her Beloved (Rev 19:7).

The Supper isn't some marginal concern in Scripture, with a few cameo roles here and there in the Gospels and Paul. The Supper fulfills the main thread of Scripture and the history it tells. As we commune together in the Supper, that history becomes ours. We are knit into the biblical story as part of its ongoing unfolding.

For the Life of the World

When we have said all that, we still need to clarify why the Supper is so crucial to the formation of God's city. We need to explain why celebrating the Supper is a critical dimension of the church's response to the varied and ever-shifting crises of world history. We need to grasp that we celebrate the Eucharist for the life of the world.

In one sense, the answer is obvious: *Jesus* is the solution to the impotence of the church and the darkness of the world. When you communicate Jesus through the word to the people of God, you're offering the solution, the *only* solution, to this battered, sinful world. A congregation who eats and drinks at the Lord's table participates in the body and blood of Christ. Our union with Jesus is deepened. We are conformed to His death and share in His resurrection. We drink the Spirit and so are equipped to serve Jesus when we disperse.

We who share the loaf and cup become one body with Christ our Bridegroom (1 Cor 10:16-17). We go out as limbs and members and organs of the Lord Jesus. We go out as an extension of Christ in the world.

But we can say more. Many Christians have described the Supper as a "Eucharist," "thanksgiving," a name derived from Jesus' prayers of thanksgiving for the bread and wine (cf. Matt 26:27; Matt 15:36; Mark 8:6). When we share this Eucharistic meal, we're united with Jesus in His one great thanksgiving to the Father, offered in His cross and resurrection. United to Christ, we're formed by the Spirit to live lives of continuous thanksgiving for all things in all circumstances.

That's the only sane way to live. All that we have is gift, and so the only rational stance in life is one of constant thanks for the gift of every breath, every heart-beat, every good and perfect gift that comes from above. Sharing Eucharist, we become a different sort of people, a *grateful* people in the midst of a humanity that, like Adam, does not acknowledge God as God or give thanks (Rom 1:18-32). A thankful people is a people attuned to reality, reality as a gift of the Father through the Son and Spirit. By the Eucharist, we become a people that models genuine human life before the world.

The Supper has a horizontal as well as a vertical dimension. In it, the Spirit unites us to the Son of the Father; in it, the Spirit also unites us to one another. We participate in the body and blood of Christ as we eat and drink; we also become one body as we partake of one loaf (1 Cor 10:16-17). Through the Supper, the church becomes who she is—the new humanity united in the Son by the Spirit; the one people constituted from every tribe, tongue, people, and nation; the people of Easter and Pentecost. By common participation in the meal, we become the city that we are called to be.

We might say that the Supper depicts the redeemed human society that is the city of God. "Depict" is too weak. The Supper isn't merely a visible sign of an invisible society. The church gathered at the Supper *is* the city of God, more and more a living sign of the perfected city to come. At the Supper, the church is a sign that accomplishes what it signifies: Sharing bread, we signify the future city and *are* that future city in the present.

This cannot but be a rebuke to the Babelic cities of men. Every time we portray the heavenly city in the Supper, we call attention to the injustice, violence, greed, and wickedness of the earthly city. Every time we celebrate the Supper, we are reminded of our *own* evils and violence and are called to repentance. Through celebration of this meal, we become a city of witness, a witness against the fallen city because we are a witness to the city that is to come.

The cities of men are acquisitive, competing for scarce goods; at the table, the citizens of God's city share bread and wine, resources as infinite as the God who gives them. The cities of men are consumerist, finding their meaning in the abundance of goods; the city of God consumes the body and blood of Jesus and becomes what she eats. The cities of men marginalize the economically useless, the unborn and children, the mad and the handicapped; at the Lord's table, the city of God welcomes all sorts and conditions of men and gives more abundant honor to those without honor.

While they exclude, the cities of men congratulate themselves for their tolerance, endorsing whatever perverse pattern of life the imagination can devise; the city of God calls sinners to *repentance* so that the penitent can share in the bread of God, feasting in the Lord's presence without shame. The cities of men oscillate between an idolatrous attachment to things and Gnostic hostility to matter; at the Supper, the city of God affirms the goodness of created things and the goodness of cultural products like bread and wine, which become means of communion with the living God. (That means, note, that our work itself becomes a means of communion.)

The cities of men are divided by race, culture, language, hatreds of centuries; the city of God doesn't erase differences, but unites people of every nation in the family meal of the Father, since the Spirit makes all of them brothers in the Son. The cities of men operate by power; the citizens of the city of God, gathered at His table, display His power made perfect in the weakness of cruciform witness. In the Lord's presence, kings kneel in penitence; at the Lord's table, kings share a meal with beggars. In the liturgy, the wealthy have no special status over the poor; at the Lord's table, rich and poor, men and women, elite and ordinary share a common meal.

For Kids

Men and women . . . and *children*. The children of the church should be included in the meal of the church.

Under Torah, there were various meals with various rules of access. Priests alone could eat most holy sacrificial food; their families were allowed to eat certain portions that no one else could eat; some food was available to anyone, priests and non-priests, who was in a state of purity (Lev 22).

No meal, however, included adult non-priests and excluded their children. Whenever an Israelite adult feasted before the Lord—at Passover, Pentecost, the Feast of Booths, with a peace offering at non-festival times—he brought his children along so that they could eat and drink and rejoice, "you and your children and your stranger who is within your gates" (Deut 12; 16).

Nothing in the New Testament changes this. If anything, Jesus intensifies the church's reception and love of children, by placing small children in the midst of His disciples as object-lessons, by welcoming the little children to His lap.

Paul's exhortations in 1 Corinthians 11 don't change this. Corinthians didn't become unworthy because they didn't have the right theology of the real presence or because they were too young to answer catechism questions. They were unworthy because of their divisiveness, because they brought their petty factions to the table of unity. Paul exhorts the Corinthians to reconcile with one another before sharing the meal of reconciliation with God. Nothing in 1 Corinthians 11 excludes children from the Lord's table. Small children are as capable of being at peace with their parents, siblings, and friends, as adults are.

Before you eat dinner, you wash your hands. For us, this is a matter of hygiene. For ancient Jews, it was a matter of ceremonial purity. Unclean Israelites were excluded from the courts of the sanctuary and its feasts, but the Lord kindly gave Israel rituals for cleansing. By washing his or her body and clothing, an unclean person is made clean, fit for an appearance in Yahweh's presence and at His table (Lev 12—15; Num 19). To use a Thomistic formula, the rites of purity were "ordered to" festivity.

In the new covenant, all those washings are concentrated in the single cleansing rite of baptism, which is as once-for-all as the cross of Jesus. Baptism doesn't just cleanse for a moment or for a few weeks. Baptism's power doesn't leak out over time. Because of his one baptism, the sinner is cleansed throughout his life, qualified to enter the presence of God, washed up for the meal.

The Supper isn't a bare sign of communion with Christ in the Spirit. It's the *event* of communion and a real present of the future city of peace. In the same way, baptism isn't a sign of an incorporation that takes invisibly, somewhere else. Baptism is the *event* of incorporation, an act of Jesus and His Spirit by which the Father adopts a person as a son or daughter. Baptism grafts the baptized into the body of Christ and makes him a priest in the temple of the Spirit. A baptized person might prove a wayward son, a cancer in the body, an unholy priest. But baptism is a gift of membership, the cleansing and sanctifying rite that makes saints.

We can close the logical circle: If children belong at the table, if we're to rejoice at the feast of the kingdom with our sons and daughters, then they've got to be washed up. If our children belong at the table of the Father, if they participate in the body and blood of the Lord, if they share the holy things as living stones in the temple of the Spirit, then they should also receive the effective sign of baptism.

The role of children in the church divides Baptistic Christians from others. It's not a minor issue. Whether we baptize babies or not, we're making a statement about the boundaries of the city of God. And not just a statement: The way we baptize, whom we baptize, shapes the kind of city we are.

Without children, the church is a club for the religiously mature. Without children, the feasts of the church are more restrictive than the feast of old Israel, as if God's hospitality had, unthinkably, contracted after the coming of the Son and Spirit. Without children, the church cannot be the new humanity that extends as far as the old humanity, from the cradle to the deathbed. Without children, the church is something less than the city of God. Without children, it may be a city under judgment, a city without children laughing in the streets and playing in the squares.

Liturgy: It's, you know, for kids.

Spiritual Weapons

So far, we've been talking about the *in*direct effects of the liturgy on the world. So far, the "target" of the liturgy has been the church. Through the word, the Lord forms a people that lives within the biblical story, teaches His promises and commands, convicts and encourages. At the table, we're formed into one body by the Spirit as we eat one loaf and receive one cup. The liturgy gathers the heavenly city on earth, and through the liturgy we become more and more the city we're called to be.

The Spirit employs word and table to form us into the city of God that renews the cities of men.

Without this—without a ministry of word and bread—the church is hungry and blind, stumbling in darkness. And a church in the darkness cannot be a light to the world. Through liturgical practice, we acquire new skills—skills of praise, prayer, thanksgiving, the skill of reading our world in biblical terms. These skills give us new powers of perception: We see what others cannot see, like the just hand of God in the collapse of a city, the shattering power of children singing, the glory of God in a crucified man.

Yet the liturgy also has a *direct* effect on the world because the citizens of God's city are also citizens and actors in earthly cities. If the liturgy changes *us*, it changes the way we live outside the liturgy. Or, to put it otherwise: For Christians, the whole city is a sanctuary, and all of life is liturgy. Monday through Saturday is an outflow and extension of Sunday, and the liturgy of the Lord's day imprints itself on week and work days.

Let's be concrete. A politician hears a sermon about justice for the poor, and he begins drafting legislation to assist them. A prominent businessman has succeeded by cutting corners, but after a sermon on Zaccheus, he repents and begins making restitution to the people he cheated. Hearing a sermon on loving one's neighbor, a manager in an auto plant changes the way he deals with his employees; an assembly line worker in the same plant is convicted of his ingratitude and laziness and strives to be a productive worker.

A politician shares the Lord's table with a homeless family, and is inspired to seek remedies for homelessness in his city. Recognizing that the Eucharist calls him to a life of generosity, a Scrooge sets up a charitable foundation. That plant manager realizes that he should stop abusing the Lord's table companions, and that assembly line worker realizes that thanksgiving should extend to his daily work.

In short, the liturgy never simply targets the church. Even when it targets the church, it targets the church for the sake of the world. The liturgy brings us into contact with God, gives us a taste of future and heavenly things, shines on us the light of the future city. But we receive light to *give* light, to be like Moses, reflecting the glory we have seen to those around us, back into the cities of men. That glory will blind some; the aroma of Christ in us will smell like death to some (2 Cor 2:14-16). Citizens of the cities of men won't welcome us and may respond with hatred. But that's all to the good since it only enhances our communion in the cross of Jesus.

Besides all that, the liturgy includes moments and actions that reach beyond the walls of the church to change the world. I'm talking about prayer and praise, which may be treated together.

The church is the city of God called to carry out a mission of renewing the cities of men. The church is God's urban renewal project. We can't do this from our own resources because we have none. W have only what has been given. *God* renews the cities of men, and the church is *nothing* except what she receives from Jesus and His Spirit. She is nothing unless she is the body of the risen Christ and the temple of the Spirit. When we say "the church transforms the world," that always, *always* means "the Spirit uses the church to transform the world."

This is why prayer is so crucial to the church's role in the world. Prayer draws us near to God. Prayer exercises and increases faith. Prayer is one part of an ongoing conversation with the God who speaks. But in Scripture, prayer is most often a request for God to act. Prayer arises from dissatisfaction with the status quo. It's an appeal to God to change the state of affairs.

In Jesus' model prayer, He instructs us to pray not only for forgiveness and daily bread, but for the world: "Hallowed be Thy name, Thy kingdom come, Thy will be done on earth as it is in heaven." When we pray that prayer (and we should, preferably singing it), we are asking God to change the world so that blasphemous persons and nations begin to sanctify God's name, so that the kingdoms of this world become the kingdoms of the Lord and His Christ, so that God's will is as readily and thoroughly obeyed here on earth as it is by angels in heaven.

Jesus' prayer is like the prayers of the Old Testament, which are frequently prayers for Yahweh to intervene into the disorder to put things in order. Psalm 2 sets the tone for the Psalter, with its vivid image of the nations in uproar and the Lord's king on Zion. Psalms often ask God to judge the earth and praise Him when He answers the prayer. A jarring number of Psalms include "imprecations," prayers that call on God to curse or destroy His enemies. Psalm 72 lays out a vision of royal justice, and Psalms 50, 82, and 94 warn that God will correct political injustice.

In this respect if in no other, the liturgy has an inescapably political edge to it. We cannot pray as the Bible instructs us without praying for God to change the world, to bring justice and peace to the nations, to cast down unjust rulers and raise up faithful ones.

Importantly, we don't merely pray for amelioration of this or that particular injustice. Injustice can be built into political and cultural systems. Evil can be enacted by decree and become so habitual that it seems normal. Most Americans, for instance, live most days without a thought to the unborn infants being slaughtered a few miles down the road. We enjoy the comforts of home while our military engages in violent adventuring on the other side of the planet.

When we pray for justice, we pray that God will bare His arm to break *systems* with a rod of iron and shatter them like earthenware. This is part of the church's urban-renewal mission: Unjust systems must be torn down so that just systems can be established. So we ask the living God of perfect justice to do just that.

If we're not praying like that, we're not praying as we ought. If we're not praying like that, we're not praying like the city of God among the cities of men.

Singing Psalms

The Psalms should be the model prayers for the church. And the church's song should center on singing Psalms. Until quite recently, it has. Christians in the New Testament sang and prayed the Psalms. From the time of St. Benedict to the present, monks sang through the entire Psalter every week. Protestants paraphrased the Psalms for congregational singing or included Psalm chants in their prayer books or wrote hymns that were based on Psalms.

Many churches today sing virtually *no* Psalms. If they sing Psalms at all, they sing a few lines, detached from context, lines that express a particular emotion but neglect the political rough-and-tumble, the anguish and desperation, that is so prominent in the Psalter.

Few items on the church's to-do list are more important than this: The Psalms must become the church's primary hymnal.

The Psalms express the full range of human experience and emotion. There are Psalms of unutterable joy ("we were like those who dream"), Psalms of ungodly anguish ("My God, My God, why have you forsaken Me?"; "darkness is my only friend"; "out of the depths I cried"), and everything in between. Without the Psalms, we're reluctant to speak openly in the presence of God. We are reluctant to be emotionally honest with God, to tell Him to His face how disappointed we are when His promises don't come to pass. Without the Psalms, we typically descend into infantile fantasizing, using worship music to buoy us up with glib happiness rather than to face the evils of the world, rather than face up to our own temptation to despair. Without the Psalms, we have no words to speak our pain, and so we are reduced to silence.

If we neglect the examples of Psalms, we would never think to sing a hymn like Psalm 83, which calls on God to turn His enemies to fertilizer ("dung" in the precious language of most English translations; better rendered as "shit"). Do these violent Psalms reek of masculine bravado? Hardly. If you're looking for some really bloodthirsty lyrics, check out the songs of Miriam (Exod 15), Deborah (Judg 5), Hannah (1 Sam 2), and Mary (Luke 1). The *Bride* of the Lamb rejoices in His victories.

Liturgical music isn't simply a matter of individual or corporate *expression*. We sing in order to fulfill and mature in our vocation as priests, kings, and prophets in Christ, the high Priest-King and chief Prophet. Music is a sacrifice of praise. Through music, we ascend in our own breath and body (not through the blood and body of an animal) to the presence of God. When we sing, we circle the cities of men with trumpets and voices, shouting until the walls fall flat (Josh 6). Faced with an invasion, Jehoshaphat called out the choir (2 Chr 20), who sang and played until the invaders were destroyed. When we as the priestly city lift up the Lord on our praises, the Lord terrorizes our enemies.

We sing as warriors of the greater David, the sweet royal singer of Israel who defeated evil spirits with a lyre and learned to fight with his fingers (1 Sam 16; Psalm 144). As we sing in the Spirit, the Spirit who gripped and clothed Gideon, Samson, Saul, David, Jesus, Peter, and Paul arms us for Spiritual war. Huguenots aroused the hatred of Catholics by marching through the streets singing Psalm 68: "God shall arise and by His might, put all his enemies to flight. In conquest shall He quell them." Like them, as we offer our breath in song, we are being prepared to offer our blood in witness. Our songs ascend so that we might follow, ascending to be enthroned with Christ in heavenly places.

When Yahweh commissioned Jeremiah, He told him that His words would plant and uproot, establish and destroy (Jer 1:10).

Jeremiah's prophetic words had divine power, the power to undo and remake worlds, the power to create and destroy. In song, we prophesy (cf. 1 Chr 25:1), shattering worlds and building new ones. If that seems like an exaggeration, think of how opera shaped radical movements in nineteenth-century Europe or of the revolutionary power of rock 'n roll, which pulled out the foundations of 1950s America and created the world that we inhabit.

The music itself must be suitable to the words. Sweet melodies have their place, but they can't carry the weight of words like Psalm 94: "Rise up, O Judge of the earth! Render a reward to the proud!" The church has her own musical tradition, which is the deep source of the tradition of Western music. Too much church music today takes its cues from pop culture, which produces commercialized music. Pop music has its place, but that place isn't in the liturgy.

Church musicians and composers should certainly write new music, updated settings for the Psalms, and hardy new hymns. But they should first immerse themselves in the Christian musical tradition.

To Theo and Thea

Theo and Thea, if you're who I think you are, you want to make a difference. You want to be part of the solution to the impotence of the church and the darkness of the world. You might be tempted to think that to do that, you need to find some outside activity, something beyond the mundane ministry of a local church. You may think you need to blog (don't! blogs are old news!), become active on Twitter and Facebook, speak at conferences, or become a political advocate and activist.

Some Christians are called to that kind of ministry. God regularly raised up "celebrity" leaders in Israel—Gideon, Samson, Samuel, David, Elijah and Elisha, Isaiah and Jeremiah.

And every believer should be alert to the many opportunities for witness outside of the local church. But you don't have to do *any* of those things to make a difference, a big difference, the biggest difference.

If you're a pastor, when you teach the Bible to the gathered people of God, preside at the Lord's table, lead the church in an ascent of praise to the throne of God, pray on behalf of the world, you are at the center of the universe. The *very* center.

If you're not a pastor, you're *still* at the center of the world every week, and your work there is as crucial as the pastor's. The liturgy is the work of the whole people. Every time you gather with other real men and women and children with real bodies as the body of Christ, the word of God that brought this world into being remakes you so that you, remade, can go out to renew the human city.

Every week, you are conformed more to the dying and living of Christ as you share His body and blood; every week, you take this dying and living out to the world. Every week, you pray that the Lord of all would bring in His justice and peace. Every week, you praise God with priestly sacrifices of song and are filled with His royal and prophetic Spirit to act and speak with Spiritual power.

Twitter *might* get you more followers, and an interview on a local newscast may serve the interests of justice. But those activities are far at the margins. The church is a city whose walls are equal in length, breadth, and width. The church is a *liturgical* city. As the *sanctuary*, Jerusalem is the center of the world, and those who are called to serve and receive God's word and God's food, those who sing and pray in the presence of the King, perform the most important activity known to man. The Spirit equips us with His power so that we go out from the sanctuary to kill and to heal, to destroy and to make alive.

3   CITY OF LIGHT

"And the city has no need of the sun or of the moon
to shine upon it,
for the glory of God has illumined it
and its lamp is the Lamb.
And the nations shall walk by its light."
Revelation 21:23-24

The Spirit sweeps John to the top of a mountain where he can survey the heavenly city descending to earth. He's like Moses, David, and Ezekiel, prophets who glimpse the heavenly pattern that is to be fulfilled on earth. He relays that vision to the first-century church, to the seven churches of Asia and the believers in Jerusalem and Rome who are beginning to feel the earth quaking beneath their feet.

Like Moses, David, and Ezekiel, he relays that vision in language. To realize the ideal city, the church has to conform to a pattern of *words* (2 Tim 1:13).

This is the essence of what's called "typology." It's not merely a way of reading the Bible, but a theology of history and a claim about the relationship of heaven and earth. Heaven is the original, the "archetype." God created earth according to the pattern of heaven so that from the very beginning, creation is a copy or "ectype" of heaven. At the beginning, the copy isn't completely conformed to the original. It's like a child's drawing, and it's supposed to become more and more like the archetype. God placed Adam and Eve in the world to glorify it so that it fulfills its destiny as a copy of heaven. Through godly human action, the heavenly archetype presses itself, like a signet on a glob of wax, onto earth.

The world matures through words. It matures as God speaks and His people hear and obey. As we receive and believe the living, creative word of the Creator, we're conformed to Jesus, the heavenly man (1 Cor 15). When we live as doers of Jesus' word, the world itself is conformed to heaven. Our prayer is answered: God's will is done on earth as it is in heaven. God does it, but He does it through us.

John expresses this in his vision through the imagery of light. The word of God created light (Gen 1:3-4) because the word *is* light (Ps 119:105). Ultimately, the Word of God is God, the God who is with God, the Word that is the life and light of men (John 1:1-5). That's the light that illumines the city, the light of the glory of God and the Lamb (Rev 21:23).

Because the Word dwells in the city, because the words of the Word are spoken in the city, the city shines with light. When the citizens of the heavenly city keep the commands of Jesus, we become light that shines before men and brings glory to the Father. Full of obedient citizens, the city is a light on a hill (Matt 5:14-16), and the nations are drawn to the light and walk in the light (Rev 21:24). Isaiah's vision of Zion is behind John's description of the city. In Isaiah, it's the Torah that beams out to draw the nations and turns them peaceable (Isa 2:1-4).

Only as the city of the Word can the city of God serve and transform the cities of men.

New Jerusalem fulfills Jesus' urban renewal project only if we are a city guided by the light. Let's think through this, starting with basics.

The God Who Speaks

God speaks. That's one of the most fundamental teachings of the Bible. God speaks on the first page of Scripture, speaks a world into existence and then commissions creatures, issues commands, pronounces judgments and curses.

When we get to the New Testament, we discover that Word isn't something secondary to the life of God. The God of the Bible wasn't a God of eternal silence before He spoke the *fiat lux*. In the beginning was the Word, and the Word was toward God, and the Word was God (John 1:1-3). The God of the Bible doesn't *happen* to speak. He is Himself, eternally and essentially, *Word* and *Breath* as well as Speaker.

God speaks *human*. He addresses human beings in human language. We don't know what kind of communication occurs in the eternal conversation that is the Father, the Word, and the Breath. But we know God can communicate with human beings. We don't know what language God spoke when He told Adam and Eve to be fruitful and multiply and fill the earth, or when He prohibited Adam from eating the fruit of the tree of knowledge, or when He told Adam that he would eat by the sweat of his brow and Eve that her pain in childbirth would be multiplied. We do know He spoke a language they understood.

The Word became flesh and dwelt among us, living a fully human life from womb to tomb and beyond. Long before, the Word entered into human discourse, speaking to Adam, Cain, Noah, Abraham, Hagar, Isaac, Jacob, Joseph, Moses, Gideon, Samuel, David, Solomon, Jeremiah, Ezekiel, Daniel. He doesn't speak some esoteric perfect language. To humans God speaks human.

God's human speech can be recorded in written form. Yahweh Himself wrote on tablets of stone with the finger of His Spirit (Exod 31:18), and Jesus the incarnate Word wrote in the dust (John 8:6). More often, God's speech takes written form as the Spirit carries saints to record God-breathed words (2 Pet 1:20-21). Some Christians want to distinguish the words of Scripture from the thoughts God wishes to communicate. According to this view, the ideas Scripture communicates are from God, but the words are human words. Paul won't have any of this: The *Scriptures*, he says, are breathed out and so are useful for every good work. The *writings* come from God, and so they are reliable and true, sufficient to equip the man of God for every good work (2 Tim 3:16-17).

The *writings* come from God, and that means the forms and patterns of Scripture are part of the truth God communicates. We need to pay attention to the structures of Scripture, the recurring narratives, the twists and turns of its poetry, its puns and metaphors. The form of Scripture isn't a human carrier of the divine word. The form is God's word to us.

Some Christians say that the Bible speaks truth in relation to "spiritual" realities but is an unreliable witness to history, the sciences, or the social sciences. A quick glance at the Bible will show that this is a ruse. It's very, *very* difficult to find anything in Scripture that deals with exclusively "spiritual" or "heavenly" realities. On the face of things, the Bible purports to be about history, *this* world, real human beings in real human situations, human beings in relation to God, the Creator and Lord of the covenant. Scripture includes a chronology of the ancient world, one that runs from the creation right through the ministry of Jesus and the apostles. The Bible describes events in the history of Israel, in which Israel often intersects with other ancient peoples. It focuses on a particular piece of land with hills and rivers and seas and cities that can be found on maps.

If the Bible is an unreliable witness to history, then it's unreliable full stop, and we ought to can it.

Some Christians worry that we can't express the ineffable realities of God in human language. In the nature of the case, they say, human talk distorts the infinite God; at best, human language gives us only the slightest glimpses of God as He truly is. We can be far more confident about what God is *not* than about who or what He *is*.

There's a bit of truth here. We don't know all there is to know about God, and never will. But that doesn't imply He can't reveal Himself truly in human language. To doubt that God can speak truly to us is another manifestation of the old nature/supernatural dichotomy I discussed in chapter 1. It assumes that creation is an obstacle to God's efforts to communicate with us, a veil that screens off God from His creatures. It's as if God's speech gets distorted as soon as it begins to vibrate the air with sound waves, as soon as it takes the form of ink marks on parchment.

That's not the biblical view of God's speech and its relation to created media. God created the world to manifest His glory. That's what the universe *is*, a created radiance of the uncreated glory of God. Creation isn't a veil between God and us; at its deepest essence, it's a *vehicle* of communication. God created the vibrating air; as Lord of air, He can shape it to His purposes, shape it to communicate exactly what He wants to communicate. God the Word created a speaking world, which speaks of him. And God the Word speaks into that speaking world.

Sola Scriptura

I'll come back to this point about creation, which is an exceedingly important one for understanding both the Bible and creation. For now, let me pursue another point: God's words are the words of the *Lord*. If God speaks and writes, then those spoken and written words carry the authority of the speaker and writer. It won't do to say, "I honor the authority of my parents, my pastor, my government, but I don't have to obey what they *say*."

Authority is *always* exercised through words. Honoring authority *means* honoring the words that authorities speak. If we bow to the authority of God the Lord, then we bow to the authority of His Word. His Word is the ultimate Word, bearing ultimate authority. If anything contradicts the Lord's Word, it must be false. Every other authority has to submit to the authority of the Word of God.

This conviction is the basis for the Reformation's dispute with Rome. It's the essence of *sola scriptura*. The Reformers didn't reject other authorities. They acknowledged the authority of the church fathers, of the church's creeds and traditions, of the church's liturgical heritage, of the church's pastors, as well as the authority of rulers outside the church—parents, kings, masters. But they insisted that *all* these authorities had to submit to the higher authority of the Word of God. No matter how venerable the tradition, no matter how widely believed or practiced, if it contradicted the Word of God, it had to be changed.

Augustine might have defined "justification" as "making-just," but if that's not what Paul meant, then even the most august of church fathers has to be corrected. Aquinas defended transubstantiation and the veneration of the consecrated Host, but if those don't measure up to Scripture, they must be revised or discarded.

Sola scriptura isn't naïve about the role of human interpretation. God speaks human, and the human language He speaks and writes has all the possibilities and limits of human language. Biblical Hebrew and Greek aren't magic languages that somehow elude the ambiguities and gnarled knots of normal human languages. We don't come to understand God's written word by a sudden bolt from the sky. We study the text, unearth what we can about the language and historical context of the text, puzzle over the oddities and inescapable ambiguities in the text, listen to and debate with others, including ancient brothers who read the same Scripture we do.

To say that interpretation is necessary, though, isn't to say we can never know what the text means. To say that interpretation is necessary doesn't mean that the interpretive process is a barrier God can't break through. We must interpret, but that obvious fact doesn't undermine the basic reality: When God speaks human to humans, He communicates. His Word gets through. Through our study, prayer, meditation, debate, with all our limits and errors, the Spirit who carried the writers carries the church to understanding.

Sola scriptura is ultimately a statement about Jesus' Lordship over His church. The question is this: Can Jesus speak to His Bride to correct and guide her? Or are all the words that the church hears simply the words of the Bride? Are preaching, theology, commentary, teaching no more than different ways in which the Bride talks to herself? Is the church's speech a monologue or a dialogue?

In the midst of history, the Bridegroom's voice is contested. The Bride talks back, and there are plenty of pretenders to the Bridegroom's role, slick serpentine suitors who would seduce the Bride. In the midst of history, the Bride's hearing is partial and self-interested. She tends to hear only the voices she wants to hear.

But the question remains: In the midst of all this, does the Bridegroom have an independent voice? Can the Spirit speak to and in the church? Once the question is put this way, we can again see that this question comes back to the old nature/supernatural problem. To say that human interpretation *prevents* Jesus from addressing His church is to say that nature is closed to the Word that comes from beyond nature. Or, it's to say that God cannot overcome the Bride's deafness. That's to say that Jesus is not the healer He seems to be. And that's to say that the kingdom has not come, and we are still in our sins.

Sola scriptura is a confession that Jesus is Lord. As Lord, He must be able to correct and renew His church by His Word. He must have an independent voice in the church. That voice is the voice of Scripture, the written word in which we hear what the Spirit of Jesus says to the churches.

Scripture and Protestant Traditionalism

Ask the Reformers. They'll tell you that clinging to the authority of the Word isn't always safe. It's dangerous to challenge long-held traditions in the name of God's word. It can get you crucified.

This is one reason why Protestants, while professing *sola scriptura*, don't always practice it. Protestants too can become traditionalists, as locked into our confessions as Catholics are to the papacy and the magisterium. If we're serious about *sola scriptura*, we need to ask questions like: Is it possible that the Reformers didn't grasp everything that the Bible says about justification? Is it possible that we may discover new things in Paul's letters, things that the Reformers missed? Is it possible that we've gained fresh insight into Scripture over the past five centuries?

Even when Protestants get things right, our theology is often guided by extra-biblical categories. Debates about the Eucharist, for instance, often become philosophical debates about the real presence, which explore the nature of symbolism, the relation of matter and Spirit or of heaven and earth, the semantic question of what "is" means in "This is my body."

Those are important questions, and we need to address them. But the Bible doesn't present the Lord's Supper in these categories. Paul never forgets that the Supper is a *meal*, celebrated by the church. He never uses a zoom lens to focus on the bread and the wine, as if they could be isolated from the people who are eating and drinking.

The Bible sets the Lord's Supper in the context of a rich theology of food, one that begins with Adam in the garden, runs through Abraham's meal with God through the Passover and the manna and the feasts of Israel, to the promise of a feast spread on Zion, a promise fulfilled in the movable feast that is the ministry of Jesus. These biblical events, categories, and images provide the categories for our understanding and practice of the Supper. We get closer to the base-line level of the Supper's reality when we say, "We feast like Mephibosheth at David's table" than when we say, "A sacrament is a visible sign of an invisible grace" (something the Bible never asserts).

This is one illustration of a more general point: Theologians often treat the Bible as if it were a collection of raw data to be mined, polished, and organized into a system of theology. Preachers treat the Bible as a book of illustrations and moral principles. We read the Bible as if it were a sacred version of Aesop's fables, full of stories designed to illustrate doctrine or to set an example for Christian living or, these days, to illustrate the single message that God's grace extends to wretches like Noah, Abraham, Isaac, Jacob, Samson, and David. This last reading is a profound *mis*reading: Noah, Abraham, Isaac, and, yes, Jacob, Jephthah, Samson, and David are heroes of *faith* (Heb 11). If they're examples, they're chiefly examples of how we *ought* to live.

Even if we interpret these stories correctly, though, it's a mistake to treat the Bible as a collection of moralizing tales. If we do that, we miss the main thrust of Scripture. The Bible is a record of public history, from creation and fall to the consummation when the Bridal city completes her procession from heaven to earth. That historical, *this*-worldly focus should be reflected in the way theologians go about theology and in the way pastors go about their teaching and preaching. The emphases of Scripture should be the emphases of our teaching and preaching.

I affirm predestination, but the Bible says a great deal more about politics than it does about predestination. I believe believers enter heaven at death, but the Bible teaches a lot more about animals than it does about the heavenly state. If we're going to preach, teach, and write about the Bible as it is, we'll have to say a lot more about land, gardens, sex, bodies, architecture, barrenness and birth, death and impurity, war and geopolitics than we normally do. We'll have to unlearn the habit of spiritualizing the visceral contents of Scripture.

We need to allow ourselves to be confronted and corrected by the Bible. We should submit to the Bible and strive to hear *what* it says to us, *how* it says it. We should strive to make Scripture's emphases our own and to let the Bible speak on its own terms rather than forcing it to speak in the idioms and patterns that we're used to. The Spirit unmakes us, including our speech and thought, so that He can put us back together. Don't resist the un-making. Don't quench the Spirit.

Of course, there are *always* heresies to confront, always false teachings to battle. Historically, much of the church's theology and teaching has focused on contested issues—the Triune nature of God, the relation of divine and human in Jesus, the way of justification, the nature of sacraments and the church. Of course, those are still proper topics for theologians and pastors to teach, for Christians to study. But we shouldn't think that we've mastered the Bible when we've mastered these contested questions. And we shouldn't let our diet of Scripture be restricted to passages that deal with those issues.

In our day, the perversions and confusions surrounding sexuality are one of the major battlegrounds for the church.

False teaching about male and female, transgenderism, sodomy and lesbian sin, abortion, and extra-marital sex must be combatted head-on. A theologian or pastor who dodges these issues is unfaithful.

But we need to resist the temptation to fight these battles with a few key texts, while missing the Bible's overall teaching. We need to study to discover what the Bible's actual teaching is on these subjects, working within biblical categories and patterns rather than from cultural assumptions, philosophy, social science data, or pressing culture-war questions.

A huge swathe of the Bible is about sex—from the creation of man as male and female and the invitation to become one flesh, through the laws of the Torah and the escapades of various kings and the allegories of the Song of Songs and the prophets, through the ministry of Jesus to women and His rescue of His Bride, with whom He becomes one flesh, to the consummation in the marriage supper of the Lamb, when the Bride and Bridegroom are joined forever. If we want to cultivate healthy Christian sexuality, we need to grasp as much of that as we can.

The Bible Speaks to Everything

Scripture carries God's own authority, which is why the Psalmist of Psalm 119 virtually worships the Torah (v. 48). *All* of Scripture is God's authoritative word to His people and to the world. We're not allowed to skip what we think of as the boring parts or the parts that we find difficult. We'll miss some essential teaching about worship if we skim lightly over Leviticus. We won't understand how to apply the Ten Commandments without working through the Book of the Covenant, Leviticus, the laws of Numbers, the book of Deuteronomy. We won't grasp what Revelation is talking about unless we have spent a lot of time in the numbingly detailed final chapters of Ezekiel.

The authority of Scripture isn't limited. We can't squeeze what Scripture teaches into some narrow category we think of as "religious" or "spiritual." The Bible is authoritative about everything it touches on, and it touches on everything.

Scripture makes claims about the origins of the universe: God created the heavens and the earth by His Word, over the course of a week. It makes claims about ancient history: Abraham left Ur in Chaldea to follow the call of God. It makes claims about human beings: We are good creatures of God, created as male and female, called to rule other creatures; through one man's transgression, sin entered the world, and death through sin, so that all sinned. We are created lower than the angels, but in Christ have been elevated above angels.

The Bible makes claims about linguistic, cultural, and religious diversity: Babel was a crucial episode in this history. The Bible makes claims about politics: A large chunk of the Old Testament amounts to a political history of Israel, Paul talks about the "powers that be," and John sees the Roman empire revealed as a terrifying beast from the sea.

When we formulate our opinions about political issues, we reason from Torah as well as other portions of Scripture. When a Christian politician puzzles over a policy issue, the Bible speaks authoritatively to it. Our understanding of the purpose of wealth, the nature of property, our responsibility to the poor and immigrants, and the limits and aims of property have to be guided by what the law, prophets, Jesus, and apostles say about wealth (which is a great deal).

The Bible doesn't tell us how to build a widget, but it tells us a lot that informs our widget-building. It tells us *why* we labor, teaches us to devote our widget-building energies to serving our neighbor, commands us to be honest in our widget-building, requires us to love the widget-builders beside or under us. Sometimes the Bible's instruction is very general:

Whatever you do, whether you eat or drink, do all to the glory of God (1 Cor 10:31). Sometimes, it's very specific: If someone slaps you on the right cheek, turn the other cheek (Matt 5:39). General or specific or somewhere between, Scripture speaks to all people in every circumstance.

There is nothing in human life outside the authority of Scripture. If Jesus is Lord of all, He governs *all* by His Word. That means there is no space that's safe from a turf war between Jesus and other authorities. Scripture challenges the status quo, calling for repentance, calling us to die and rise. If Jesus is Lord of all, there are no Scripture-free zones.

Things Concerning Jesus

At the heart of the Theopolitan vision is a way of reading, studying, and teaching the Bible. Scripture has a universal scope. In it, God speaks with authority to all of human life—what we are to believe, how we are to live as individuals and as societies, what we are to expect in the future.

But the Bible has a focal point, a center. It's a record of human history, centered on the history of Israel. That history comes to a climax in the life, death, and resurrection of Jesus. Jesus is the principal character of Scripture. The Bible is *His* story, and His life is the hinge of the ages, *the* turning point of world history.

Scripture's single, complex history can be disentangled into three strands. It is a story of *redemption*: Adam sinned and was cast from the garden, but God promised a Savior. God called Abraham and chose Israel to be an instrument of redemption, to bring the savior into the world. After a long and uneven history, God fulfilled His promise by sending Jesus, who gave Himself on the cross for the sins of the world and was raised for our justification.

The story of the Bible is also a story of *holy war*. God placed Adam in the garden to guard and tend it. Adam failed when he allowed the serpent to seduce and deceive Eve. Adam's sin was a failure to make war on the serpent. But God promised a Seed who would crush the serpent's head, a son of Adam who would be a faithful holy warrior.

Throughout the Old Testament, the Lord sent many saviors to rescue Israel, His Bride: Moses, Joshua, Gideon, Samson, David, Hezekiah, Josiah. But these dimly foreshadowed the Holy Warrior who was still to come. Jesus combats Satan directly, in the wilderness and at the cross, when the prince of this world is cast out. Because of Jesus, Satan falls from heaven like lightning, and the dragon falls to the earth. Jesus gathers an army to battle alongside Him, head-crushers and giant-killers, who carry on His holy war until the end of the world, when the dragon, the serpent of old, will finally be thrown into the lake of fire.

The Bible is also a story of *maturation*, the growth of humanity from Adamic infancy to new-Adamic maturity. Adam was a newborn when he was placed in the garden, not yet ready for the solid food of the tree of knowledge. He was created a priest in the garden-sanctuary, but through battle with the serpent was supposed to train as a king. Adam failed as priest and was thrown from the garden, but God's plan to raise humanity from childhood continued. God still intended to raise the children of Adam from priests to kings to prophets.

Paul says that Israel was like a minor who is heir of a great treasure (Gal 4:1-7). So long as the heir is a child, he's treated like a servant, under angelic guardians and managers, under the tutelage of the law. When the Son comes into the world, He brings the children to maturity. Jesus brings many sons to glory (Heb 2:10), to raise us onto thrones, so that we can share in His rule over the creation. Through the Last Adam, we're set on track to complete the first Adam's task of dominion. We're set back on track to grow up to mature humanity.

We can tell the story of the Bible in each of these ways and in many more. However we tell the story of the Bible, we tell it as a story of *Jesus*, of preparation for Jesus, the coming of Jesus, and the church's participation by the Spirit in the work of Jesus.

Jesus isn't just the end of the story. He's unveiled *throughout* the story. As Jesus told His disciples after His resurrection, everything in Moses, the Psalms, and the prophets concerns Him (Luke 24). The Old Testament is a complex tapestry of types and shadows of Jesus in His suffering and glory.

Every major *protagonist* of the Old Testament reveals something of Jesus. Jesus is the Last Adam, the head of a renewed human race. Jesus suffers at the hands of His brothers as Abel died at the hand of Cain. Jesus is the true Seed of Abraham, the true Isaac, who dies and rises. Jesus is the new Joseph, who suffers in patience until He is exalted to rule and give bread to the hungry world. Jesus is Joshua, conquering the land. Jesus is a new warrior king like David, a sage on the throne like Solomon, a child-king rescued from death like Joash. He is the rebuilder of the temple, like Joshua and Zerubbabel, the builder of city walls like Nehemiah.

Every *office* and *institution* of the Old Testament foreshadows Jesus. Jesus is a priest of the order of Melchizedek, a priestly order superior to the fleshly priesthood of Aaron (Heb 7). Jesus is great King David's greater Son. Jesus is a miracle-working prophet like Elisha and a weeping prophet of doom like Jeremiah. Jesus tabernacles in human flesh, and His body is the temple. Jesus' death is a sacrifice, fulfilling all the offerings of the Levitical system.

The Old Testament doesn't merely give us momentary snapshots of Jesus, but also records sequences of events that foreshadow the life and ministry of Jesus. Again and again, Old Testament characters experience an exodus. They're exiled from the land, prosper in the midst of oppression, and finally escape slavery with much plunder. Abraham, Jacob, Moses himself, and David all experience exodus. Israel goes through two exoduses, from Egypt and then from Babylon. Luke tells us that Jesus comes to lead an exodus (Luke 9:31), which leads from sin and death but also from the doomed people of Israel. Martyrs above the firmament sing the song of Moses, having experienced an exodus from earth to heaven (Rev 14—15). The disciples of Jesus troop out of Judaism as Israel marched from Egypt, bearing the oracles of God as plunder.

What I've been describing is what is traditionally called "typological" reading of Scripture. It's analogous to the literary technique of "foreshadowing." Early in a novel, an author drops hints of later episodes. God, who writes with events and not merely with words, foreshadows the final act in earlier acts. The New Testament writers read the Old Testament this way, as a foreshadowing of what God has done in Jesus and through the church. We should learn our method of interpretation from the apostles.

Sometimes, though, typology becomes a method for transposing the earthly and historical events of the Old Testament into a "heavenly" and "spiritual" key: Old Israel was a polity, but the church is a "spiritual" reality. The exodus was an earthly rescue, but it foreshadowed the "spiritual" salvation Christians experience.

That way of reading is another manifestation of the old nature/supernatural dichotomy: The Old Testament is about "natural" Israel, and the New Testament is about "supernatural" salvation.

That's not how the Bible works. Jesus is just as material as Moses. His death is as real as any Old Testament sacrifice. The salvation He achieves is as this-worldly as the rescue of Israel from Egypt or Babylon. Jesus rescues from Satan and sin. But sin shapes systematic cultural and political systems, what Paul calls "principalities and powers." Jesus delivers from social malfunctions, political oppression, cultural perversions and incorporates us into the realm of the Spirit who forms the social body of new Jerusalem, God's city.

Nor is typology some effete aesthetic imposed on, and designed to evade, the hard realities of history. To read the Bible that way would again manifest a nature/supernatural dichotomy. Typology isn't a literary device, a flourish on the factual surface of the text. Typology is about the shape of history. Typology isn't just about the *telling* of history. A typological reading unveils the pattern in the tapestry of historical events themselves.

God works in regular patterns. Again and again, history runs through a similar sequence—a pattern of seven, a movement of exile-and-exodus, death-and-resurrection, fall-judgment-decline-final judgment-recreation, separation and reunion. As we read the Bible, we develop a feel for the rhythms of history, which are God's rhythms.

Creation itself is a set of types and shadows of God. God speaks light into existence, light that makes visible the eternal light that He is. He shapes light into sun, moon, and stars so that these physical realties manifest the light and glory of God. God creates rocks because He is the Rock of Israel; some rocks contain light. God created man as His image to more fully reveal His character.

Creation is a manifestation of the glory of God, not in some general way but in the specific ways that Scripture explains and expresses. The Bible forms us into a people who grasp reality as it is. The Bible enables us to hear the tune of the times. The Bible gives us new eyes to see reality as it truly is, as a revelation of the glory of God. The Bible enables us to live in a world of symbols, which is the *real* world.

To Theo and Thea

Theologians and Bible scholars often think that they're the primary teachers of the church. They're wrong.

Theology and biblical scholarship are ministries of the church, which means that scholars are servants of pastors, preachers, and people. Theology doesn't come to its climax in a plenary lecture at the Society of Biblical Literature or in a paper published in *Modern Theology* or in a widely-reviewed book that wins a *Christianity Today* award. Theology and biblical scholarship come to their climax in the liturgical assembly of the people of God, where a pastor delivers the word of the Lord to the people of God at the Lord's table.

To you theologians and scholars, remember that you serve the church, its pastors and its people. And to those Theos who are pastors, theologians exist for *your* sake, to assist you as you do the really big work of theology. Don't let them belittle you.

And to you Theos and Theas in the pew: The whole apparatus of Bible study and teaching is for *you* so that you can be shattered and reborn by the hammer of God's Word. The Word of God is the light of God, and everything that comes into light is light (Eph 5:13). If you receive the light of the Word, you're being made over into a light source. As you obey the word, your good works shine before the nations.

New Jerusalem can be a city of light only if *you* are lights, witnesses through the Spirit in suffering and glory. New Jerusalem draws and guides the nations only if *you* are lit by the Word.

You want to make a difference, a big difference, the biggest difference? Hear the word, believe the word, sing the word, speak the word, obey the word, and the Spirit will ignite you as the city of light shining out in the darkness.

4 ANGELS AT THE GATES

It had a great and high wall
with twelve gates,
And at the gates twelve angels.
Revelation 21:12

God formed Adam from the ground and placed him in a garden east in the land of Eden. Yahweh told him to "guard" and "serve" the garden (Gen 2:15). We find out later in the Bible that "guard duty" and "service" are Levitical and priestly responsibilities (cf. Num 1:53; 3:10; Deut 10:8). Adam was a priest in the garden, a watchman who protected Eve and the garden itself from intruders.

When Moses built a tent-garden at the foot of Sinai, Aaron, his sons, and the Levites took up Adamic guard duty. Non-priests and unclean people had to be kept away from the house of Yahweh. If the house got polluted, Yahweh would abandon it and leave Israel as prey to vicious Gentiles.

In the new covenant, that Adamic-Aaronic task belongs *especially* to pastors. In John's vision of new Jerusalem, there are "angels" at the gates. They permit kings to bring in their treasures

(Rev 21:24) but screen out impurity and abominations (21:27).

Earlier in Revelation, Jesus sends messages to the "angels" of the churches of Asia (Rev 2—3). These *must* be pastors and overseers rather than spiritual beings: Why would Jesus *write* to spiritual angels? From those messages, we see that Jesus holds the angels responsible for the state of the church. The angels should drive out the Balaamites and followers of Jezebel. They need to deal with the Nicolaitans. They need to keep the churches faithful, to awaken the drowsily complacent Laodiceans who are neither hot nor cold.

In John's final vision, the angels are also human beings, shepherds who guard the flock, watchmen who keep the city, even to the point of laying down their lives.

New Jerusalem is a liturgical city, a city of the Word, a city of light. But she remains so only if there are angels at the gates, only if these angels are equipped and faithful.

Heirs of Aaron's Rod

The church is a real-world society of real men and women and children with real bodies and souls. This visible communion of people—the Bride and body of Christ, the family of the Father, the temple of the Spirit—is an outpost, an effective sign and real present, of the future city of God.

The future city is the new creation, a new heavens and a new earth, joined in marriage to the Lamb. As I've emphasized, new creation isn't simply future. Jesus brought salvation into the world, and that salvation takes human form as a communion of forgiven and Spirit-filled men and women and children. Heaven and earth are *already* joined, and the church is the historical form of that union. The church is salvation in historical form.

The church doesn't exist for her own sake, but for the sake of the world. The mission of the church is to be herself, God's city.

Because she is God's city, she is whisked up by the Spirit into the mission of Jesus. As new Jerusalem, she exists to bring life to the nations. She is on a mission from God, an urban-renewal mission.

The church includes evangelism in the narrow sense of proclaiming the gospel to individuals, baptizing them into the Eucharistic community, discipling them in the church, equipping them to serve the Lord Jesus. But the mission of the church is bigger and broader than that. As individuals believe the gospel and become citizens of God's city, the cities of men are transformed. As the church lives in the light of the word, the city becomes a beacon to the nations. God's light shines from the city of God into the cities of men, and whatever is in the light is light (Eph 5:13). The cities of men begin to shine, however dimly, with the glory of God and the light of the Lamb.

But that's not all. The church also exists to disciple cities and nations. As the body of Christ animated by the Spirit of Jesus, the church calls the kingdoms of this world to become the kingdoms of the Lord and of His Christ. Political, social and economic structures are to be infused with the gospel. Cultural values are to take on the shading of faith, hope, and love. The words of Scripture are to be translated into musical notes, paint, wood and stone, poetry and story. Kings and civic leaders are to imitate the humility of Jesus and, like Jesus, defend the interests of the least of their subjects.

No city in this age, in this time between the first and final Advent of the Son, will ever perfectly conform to the city to come. No human society perfectly embodies the gospel and conforms perfectly to the word of God. That includes the church, which will always be a people on the way, always beset with enemies within, always a church militant.

However imperfect, the church *is* the body of Christ, the family of the Father, the temple of the Spirit, the reality of salvation as well as a sign of a salvation to come. However partially, the cities of men that come under the influence of the church do begin to resemble the heavenly Jerusalem.

That is a breathtaking vision. I hope, Theo and Thea, that it takes your breath away. But the next step is even more breathtaking: The weapons of the church's warfare, the tools of her construction, are baptism and teaching in the Eucharistic community. Jesus gives the church a bowl of water, His commandments, a loaf of bread and a jug of wine, and then He says, "Go at it! Make disciples of the nations! Build the city of God in the world! Bring the life of the city of God to the cities of men. Renew the city. Light the nations. Suffer with Me, witness to Me, triumph in Me. You've got water, My word, bread, and wine. *What more could you possibly need?*"

This doesn't seem reasonable. If the church is going to fulfill the planetary mission of Jesus, we think, surely she needs something more than *this*. She needs a strategic plan, a lobbying consultant, a PR firm, a web site, Facebook page, a Twitter account. She needs to have some tactics for taking, holding, and wielding *real* power in the world.

Jesus isn't reasonable. He promises to go with us by His Spirit; He is the Captain of the Host, but the armies that follow Him have only spiritual weapons. The church carries out her mission to the world by bringing out the hidden treasures of God's house. The city of God transforms the cities of men by being herself, a community of word and table.

But notice that there's a third item hidden in the inner sanctuary. Along with the tablets of the law and a jar of manna is the rod of Aaron the priest (cf. Num 17). When we get to that third item, we begin to see how human beings fit into the program.

The word doesn't teach itself. Sermons don't preach themselves. The Spirit doesn't directly reveal things to every individual. God has chosen to build up His people through teachers. Jesus has chosen to address His church by equipping *pastors* to speak on His behalf.

Bread doesn't serve itself, and wine doesn't pour itself. The liturgy doesn't happen on its own. It must be *led*. At the Lord's table, someone has to take Jesus' part, blessing and breaking bread, giving thanks for the cup and passing it out.

Teaching happens all the time. Parents teach their children. Sunday school teachers teach. But there are angels in the church, pastors who are ordained to teach. If you're a pastor, you're commissioned by Jesus to teach your church everything that Jesus commanded. Other people can baptize. Sometimes, the church celebrates the Supper without a pastor. But *you're* designated and equipped by the Spirit to do these things.

Do you realize what this means? The book and the bread are the most potent powers in the world. The word of God called the universe into existence, and you get to wield the word of God among the people of God. You get to proclaim the new-creating gospel. The bread is participation in the body of Christ, and the cup is participation in the blood of Christ, and Jesus put that bread in *your* hands so you can serve Christ to the gathered people of God. The book and the bread are the most powerful weapons in the arsenal, and the Commander of the church has entrusted them to *you*.

So much depends on good pastors. Pastors are the sinews and ligaments of the body of Christ. Without pastors, the church is a flabby mess. It has no structure. It has no vision. It flounders. It cannot be God's city or carry out His mission of urban renewal.

"Pastor" means "shepherd," and in the Bible a shepherd is a *king*. Moses the shepherd did what Adam didn't: He fought off enemies and protected the bride (Exod 2:17). David—the David who defeated Goliath, drove out Philistines, was a terror to surrounding nations—David shepherded Israel (Ps 78:70-72). Yahweh is the ultimate Shepherd, who defends and leads His flock with a mighty hand. Jesus is the Good Shepherd who battles false shepherds to the point of laying down His life for the sheep. When the church has no shepherds, or weak and vacillating shepherds, she is prey to wolves, false shepherds, and dragons.

If you're not willing to confront the sins of the church and culture, don't take a step toward the pulpit. If you can't endure the backlash from your congregation or the world outside, don't pretend to preach. If you're not ready to fight, don't become a pastor. If you're a pastor and have given up fighting, repent or resign.

Or, try this picture: Paul calls himself a wise master builder (1 Cor 3:10), equipped by the Spirit, like Bezalel and Oholiab (Exod 36:1), to make God's tent. As pastor, you're a general contractor under the greater Solomon, overseeing the construction of God's city in your own city. Build with the right materials. Hay, straw, wood will be burned up as soon as God stokes a fire in the church. But if you build with gold, silver, and precious stones, the fire will just make them shine brighter.

A church without faithful pastors can't do what Jesus wants the church to do—be the city of God among the cities of men, the light to the world, the discipler of nations. Jesus is the Good Shepherd. He will guide and lead and protect His church even when wolves take over. But that's not normal practice. Normal practice is for Jesus to guide and lead and protect His church through men like you.

Pastor Theo, your calling is gigantic. What do you do?

At the Table

Every Sunday, you get to lead the people of God into the presence of God so they can hear His word and feast at His table. Every Sunday, you stand at the center of the universe, in the Most Holy Place, to bring out God's treasures. Every Sunday, you lead the church in spiritual war in preaching, prayer, song, and

Eucharist. Every Sunday, you edify (= "build") the city of God and equip the saints to carry out the urban renewal movement that is the church's mission.

Leading the liturgy has some theatrical elements to it. You need to learn to speak, move, gesture in a way that is appropriate to the occasion. Tossing off "This is the body of Christ, given for you" in a casual, perfunctory manner suggests you don't believe what you're saying.

But the liturgy *isn't* theater. You aren't *playing* at something. You're *doing* something. At the command of Jesus, you're gathering the church in the presence of God, leading them in confession, teaching them the Scriptures, and breaking bread with them, the one loaf that knits them together as the one body of Christ. You lead the church as she becomes what she is— a present outpost of the future Bridal city.

Several moments of the liturgy are critical. By a pleasing serendipity, each can be named with a word beginning with "C": Call, Confession, Consecration, Communion, Commission.

1. The *call* is the Lord's invitation for people to gather in His presence. It shouldn't be taken for granted. We can't sashay into God's presence, sipping a latte and chatting about the football game. In the liturgy, we enter the presence of the living God. He's *actually* there. He is our Father, but He is also Lord and Judge. We appear before Him, in part, to stand for inspection. It's your privilege as pastor to summon people, to extend the Father's invitation to His children, the King's invitation to His courtiers.

2. We enter the courts of the Lord with joy. We also enter His courts with fear. We know we have sinned. We know we're unclean, and need to be washed before we can come to His table. In the Old Testament, Israelites went through repeated washings. We receive only the one baptism for forgiveness of sins. But each week, that one baptismal washing is refreshed. As pastor, you have the duty to remind the congregation that they need

forgiveness. As pastor, you have the privilege to call the people of God to *confess* their sins.

That means that you have the privilege of establishing the liturgy as a zone of transparent honesty in a world of spin, scapegoating, and blame. Few things are more crucial for the health of God's city than this. The church should be one place on earth without subterfuge or dodging. It's called to be the city of truth.

It's the city of truth because it's the city of forgiveness, the city of expiations. After leading the people in confession, you have the privilege of assuring them that they *are* forgiven. You pronounce "absolution," telling those who have confessed that God has heard their prayers.

Some pastors hedge. Some liturgical traditions turn the declaration of forgiveness into a further prayer. Some are laden with conditionals that undermine assurance ("*if* you repent"— but I thought I just did!). Don't do that. Speak forthrightly. Say "I declare to you that your sins are forgiven" or, more boldly, "I, as a called and ordained servant of the Word, forgive your sins."

It's not pride. You're not forgiving by your own authority. You speak with the authority of Jesus. Speak like Jesus. He breathed His Spirit on His disciples so they could forgive sins in His name (John 20:22-23). Every believer has the same Spirit, and so each has authority to forgive sin. But you as pastor have a particular responsibility and privilege: You get to declare *public* absolution to the people of God in the public liturgy. You get to announce that the city of truth is a city of mercy.

Israel went through a series of purifications at the foot of Sinai. They washed their clothes and bathed their bodies and offered offerings. Only then did Moses ascend to the cloud. Christians still need cleansing before we ascend. That's what confession is for: If we confess our sins, God is faithful and just to forgive our sins and cleanse us from all unrighteousness (1 John 1:9-10).

3. Having been cleansed, we ascend. This is our *consecration*. In the new covenant, the one who ascends the mountain is Jesus, the greater Moses. Unlike Moses, He doesn't leave us at the foot. When He ascends, He takes us, His body, with Him. We haven't come to Sinai but to the heavenly Zion, to the assembly of angels and the hosts of heaven (Heb 12:18-24).

Somewhere in most of the historic liturgies, the pastor and congregation exchange these words: "Lift up your hearts. We lift them up to the Lord." It's a small thing, but its implications are monstrous. It's a little sign that we enter the presence of God in heaven. Like John, we hear the trumpet voice of the call, and the Spirit snatches us up to join the liturgy of the future.

This is *real*. Heaven and earth join in the liturgy. That's what makes the liturgy an effective sign of the kingdom. That's what makes the assembly of God's city a real presence of the future city. That's what makes it possible for new Jerusalem to be a light of new life among the cities of men.

This is mysterious. The liturgy is a mystical experience in the truest sense. But let's keep this concrete. What does this ascension look like? In Levitical worship, an animal was killed and dismembered, then turned to smoke. As smoke, the animal entered the presence of God, bringing a sweet-smelling savor and covering the stench of sin. We don't offer animals. Anointed by the Spirit, we're enveloped in the fragrance of Christ. In Him, *we* ascend as a sweet-smelling savor.

What do we observe as the *church* ascends? No animals, no fire or smoke. We observe the church ascending as a sweet-sounding *song*. Song is the sacrifice of praise (Heb 13:15). Song is the ladder of ascent. Israel sang "Psalms of ascent" as they walked the dusty road up to Jerusalem; so too we sing as we ascend to heavenly Zion. We sing as we process into the Most Holy Place to receive God's gifts.

At the mountaintop, the Lord speaks. That means, Pastor Theo: *You* speak. You speak in the name of the Lord. Jesus authorized you as His spokesman. You'd better stick to the script. This is such an important part of a pastor's work that I've devoted a separate section to it below.

Somewhere in the liturgy, you lead the people in prayer. Every Christian can pray, of course. But the liturgy is the act of the whole church. Pastors are ordained to act on behalf of the church. Prayer, as I've explained in chapter 2, is one of the chief weapons of our warfare, one of our chief tools for urban renewal. God hears and answers and acts on our behalf. We pray in accord with God's promises, and He keeps His promises. We ask that His justice and peace would prevail among nations. We ask that he would break the teeth of bestial men and regimes. We ask that He would avenge the blood of His saints. We pray for the peace of the city. He hears and does what we ask.

4. You're not done when you're done with the sermon. You're not done when you've offered a pastoral prayer. There's still *communion* to come. In fact, the whole service is a Eucharistic service. The whole liturgy is an ascent toward joy, the joy of the wedding feast.

You get to stand in for Jesus, the host of His table. You get to do what Jesus did. And you *should* do what Jesus did. Sometimes that means you shouldn't do what the church's liturgical tradition says you should do. Some liturgies tell you to "consecrate" the bread and wine. Some tell you to "set the elements apart" for holy use. Jesus, though, *blessed* the bread and *gave thanks* for the cup. His prayer was Eucharist, thanksgiving (Matt 26:26-27). True, Paul says that we sanctify all of God's gifts through prayer and thanksgiving (1 Tim 4:4). So Jesus did "sanctify" the bread and the wine by giving thanks. You should "consecrate" the way Jesus did, by offering thanksgiving.

Jesus prayed *two* prayers, one for the bread and one for the cup (cf. Matt 26:26-27). So should you. Jesus broke the bread, passed it out, and all ate. Jesus blessed the cup, passed it out, and all drank. Two separate prayers, two separate distributions, two separate acts of consuming.

Churches tend to mash all that together. The pastor offers only one Eucharistic prayer or dips the bread into the wine so both are consumed together. Does it matter? It mattered if an Aaronic priest reversed the order of an offering, eating his portion before offering the Lord's portion on the altar. It mattered a lot: That's one of the "great sins" that got Hophni and Phinehas killed (1 Sam 2:12-17). The God who dictated Leviticus from Sinai, the God who killed Hophni and Phinehas, took flesh in Jesus. He's the same God, with the same concern for liturgical precision. Best to be on the safe side: Do what Jesus did. Do *exactly* what Jesus did.

5. The city of God gathers for covenant renewal. The church is called into assembly, openly confesses sin and receives forgiveness, ascends in song to heavenly Zion, where she hears the word and feasts at the Lord's table. That builds the church. In the liturgy, the city of God is most fully herself. And in the liturgy, the city of God is repaired, built, glorified so that she becomes more like the city to come.

Yet the church doesn't gather for her own sake. She prays on behalf of kings and all sorts and conditions of men. She gathers in the presence of the glory to be transformed into the image of glory. The church gathers before God so that she becomes a mirror of His beauty. In the *commission and benediction*, Pastor Theo, you have the privilege of sending the people of God back out into the world, back down the mountain, to love and serve Jesus the Christ. You send them out with the blessing of God so that the church, dispersed, can carry on the urban renewal project that is our mission.

Preach the Word

Pastor Theo, if you don't know it now, you'll know it soon enough: The demands on pastors are back-breaking. You're supposed to inspire joy during festive seasons and mourn in repentance during seasons of penitence. You enter every scene of carnage—death, sickness, divorce, bankruptcy, abuse and shame—and every battlefield—husbands *versus* wives, parents *versus* children, employer *versus* employee, member *versus* pastor—and you're supposed to have something challenging or comforting to say.

All these demands can be intimidating, even overwhelming. There is no bottom to the damage your people do to themselves, to one another, to strangers, no limit to the harm they suffer. You're called to labor in the infinite abyss of human misery.

You might have trouble figuring out what you're supposed to do next, how to prioritize your time. That's why you need to keep yourself focused on the main things you are called to do and be. You are a servant of Jesus Christ, a minister of the Word and Sacraments, ordained as a leader of Christ's church to teach, preach, and lead worship. That's the way you carry out the royal office of shepherd, your role as an angel at the gates.

Your work is work in the Word. Don't let that slide. Whatever you do, don't stop reading, praying over, tarrying with, meditating on, and studying the Bible. Don't think you've got it all down because you've been to seminary. Don't think that you can have an effective, godly ministry by cutting corners, by devoting your time to what might seem more effective activities. You have one book to master, the book that is designed to master you.

You are called to teach the Bible. The *Bible*, and not some other authoritative text, not some message that would be deemed relevant by the editorial board of the *New York Times*, not anecdotes about your cuddly kids or your sex life. *The Bible*.

When you teach every Sunday, you should be teaching Scripture, explaining it to the real men and women and children who are listening.

Here's what you want to do, every Sunday: Explain what the text says, what it's about. Teach the people the basic, literal context of Scripture. Show them how the passage reveals Jesus, because everything in Scripture says something about Jesus.

Tell them how the passage affects them. They are in Christ, and so every passage that teaches about Jesus—which is *every* passage—teaches something about their lives as disciples. You don't need to come up with "Dos" or "Don'ts" every Sunday. You don't have to give them a list. But everything you teach them should affect the way they lean into and live in the world. The church's trust in the word and obedience to it constitute the best reading of Scripture. The life of the people is where the Bible comes to be real.

Sometimes you need to give them dos and don'ts. In a world where everything goes, where God's commandments are ignored, even by many Christians, you must say what the Bible says. You need to say what the Bible says even if it's controversial and politically incorrect, even if you'll get attacked.

Try this: Scripture takes for granted the reality of slavery and regulates it so that it conforms to God's justice and mercy. What Jesus said about divorce no doubt applies to slavery: It exists because of the hardness of people's hearts. Over time, the church rightly strove to abolish slavery entirely.

Yet neither Moses nor Paul is an abolitionist. The accent in Torah is on freeing slaves: Having been delivered from the house of bondage in the exodus, Israel was to imitate Yahweh in liberating slaves and the oppressed.

Otherwise, the law regulates slavery to bend it toward social goods. An indebted man works off his debt by becoming a bond-servant. That serves everyone's interests: It restores the creditor's loss. It enhances the dignity to the debtor because he is able to pay his debt. If the creditor is conscientious, he'll use the time of servitude to help his servant learn to live as a free man so that he won't slip back into slavery in the future. In six years, he has to go free, unless he wants to remain in his master's home forever.

Judged by biblical standards, American slavery was evil: Slaves were kidnapped and sold to slave traders; they weren't allowed to go free; and their masters often denied them the training and tools they needed to live as free men and women. Judged by biblical standards, most historical forms of slavery have been wicked.

But that doesn't change the facts on the page: The Bible condemns certain forms of slavery but permits others. That's what the Bible *actually says* about slavery. We should probe these passages to learn how Christians should deal with contemporary slavery (it still exists!) and to gain wisdom about how to address other social evils.

Say any of that in public, and people will stop listening and start shouting. You'll get attacked as a bigot and a racist.

Or try this: Start preaching through Leviticus 18 and 20. Most everyone will accept the rules of incest, though some will blanch when they discover that God imposed the death penalty for certain forms of incest. When you get to sodomy, you'll get everyone's attention. Yahweh calls it an "abomination" when a man lies with a man as with a woman. Paul says that same-sex passion is unnatural, a sign that God has given a culture to its destructive desires (Rom 1:18-32).

Even once-straightforward, once-commonsensical teachings of Scripture have become controversial. "Male and female created He them." "Be fruitful, multiple, fill, subdue, and rule the earth." That sounds like hate speech to many today. But the Bible says these things, and pastors must say what Scripture says.

You're angel-messengers at the gates, and you must relay the message of your Master.

Don't provoke controversy for the sake of provoking controversy. Don't exaggerate the harshness of the Bible for effect. Study hard and deeply so that you know what the text actually says. Remember when you're teaching on homosexuality or transgenderism or greed that you may have church members who battle disordered desires. Teach in a way that encourages them to overcome their shame and seek your help.

Yet, having covered all those bases, don't shy away from preaching and teaching the whole Bible, every last puzzling or appalling syllable. Everything in Scripture is about Jesus. Every word is the word of the living Word, who is the life-giving Word. Trust every word. Teach every word.

Often, you should aim your sermon at the imagination more than at the will. You don't merely want the congregation to *act* differently. You want them to see the world through Bible eyes, to recognize the patterns of history that Scripture reveals, so they can discover new and surprising paths of faithfulness.

Finally, you want to remind them of what they have to hope for. If every text reveals something about Jesus, it reveals something about what is yet to come, since Jesus is the once *and coming* King. Encourage them to hope for God's deliverance and aid in this world as well as in the next. Encourage them to expect the kingdom of God to grow into a mountain that fills the earth, to rise to be chief of the mountains, and encourage them to find ways to fit into God's great movement of re-creation. Encourage them to hope that God's city will transform the cities of men.

Whenever you pick up a Bible to teach, teach your listeners what they should believe, what they should do, what they should hope for. Teach them to seek the Spirit's fruits of faith, love, and hope.

The Catholic Pastor

Then it's Monday. Now what?

You've got to get another sermon ready. You have administrative commitments. You have Bible studies to prepare and deliver. You have members to counsel. You have coffee scheduled with an unbeliever you met during an evangelistic campaign. You have visits on your calendar. You have meetings and meetings and more meetings—meetings with the treasurer, meetings with the deacons, meetings with the elders, meetings with the pastoral staff, meetings with the pastor for meetings.

Through it all, don't lose sight of the purpose: You're an angel at the gate. You're the head of the local suburb of the heavenly city. You're there to build, repair, and guide God's city, to make it shine with the light of heaven, to make sure that refreshing water flows out. That's what all those meetings and visits are for. Don't be satisfied with preserving enough stability and peace so you can get your next sermon prepared and have evenings off. You're a city builder. You're a specialist in urban renewal. You're not a caretaker. You're called to be a culture-maker, and the first culture you cultivate is your church.

Primarily you do that through your teaching and liturgical leadership. But your teaching has to become particular and personal. You don't merely speak to the congregation on Sunday. You speak to individual men and women and children throughout the week. A lot of that conversation takes the form of encouragement, comfort in sorrow, even small talk.

Unlike lawyers or doctors, you don't have a professional area. You don't specialize in caring for their bodies, or for their legal problems, or their taxes and annuities, or for their parenting and vocation. You don't simply care for their "spiritual life" or their piety. You watch over their souls, which means you care for their *lives* in all their dimensions.

You especially watch over their souls when they're threatened with death. If you have a specialty at all, it's a specialization in death, big deaths and small deaths, the thousand natural shocks that flesh is heir to. When someone is sick, they call the doctor—and you. When a member is in legal trouble, they call the lawyer—and you. When someone loses a job, they consult with an employment agency—and you.

When a couple is having marital problems, you're the counselor of first resort. When one of the kids is drifting or rushing toward ruin, they expect you to have something to say. When an aging parent is dying, you're there with the hospice nurse. When a young woman is dying too young, you're there to weep with those who weep. In the emergency room, in the troubled home, with the battered wife or the abused child, at the lawyer's office, in court—you're there through it all.

In it all, you speak the Lord's word. You speak for Jesus. You *are* the presence of Jesus. You're called to call them to faithfulness in the midst of their anguish. You're a witness, and you're called to show them how their circumstances, no matter how devastating, present opportunities for witness.

Apart from moments of crisis, you're called to guide the members of your church to Christian maturity. You suggest how they can cultivate the gifts of the Spirit so that each becomes the fullest possible version of himself, making the fullest possible contribution to building God's city. You need to study the members of your congregation to discover their passions, interests, talents. And you should direct them toward work, within the church and without, where they can flourish.

This is one of the key ways the city of God transforms the cities of men, as pastors deploy gifted members to strategic locations in the world and guide those men and women to use their gifts effectively. As pastor, you urge members not only to ask, "How can I make a living?" or "How can I support my family?"

You urge members to ask, above all, "How can I use my gifts to do the work of Christ in the world? How can I love God and my neighbor in my vocation? How can my gifts contribute to building the city of God and renewing the cities of men?"

These aren't one-way conversations. I use the word "deploy" to capture the military dimension of the pastor's role. But of course you don't simply give orders: "You, there, you're good with numbers. You're an accountant." There is give-and-take as you help them discover their gifts. Throughout those conversations, you have an agenda—to direct their attention to asking how their gifts are gifts to the church and the world. You must keep re-directing them to this question: "How can I live and work as X in a Christ-like way?"

The members of your congregation are sent into the cities of men to disrupt, to derail the wicked ways of the world. Don't encourage them to go along to get along, to slip easily into dehumanizing and debilitating systems. Encourage them to be faithful witnesses even if they bear financial, vocational, or reputational costs as a result. Teach them to expect opposition and that the suffering they endure is a privilege of disciples. Teach them to count themselves worthy to suffer shame for the sake of Jesus. You are a witness, a martyr, leading a company of martyrs.

That's all part of the catholic vocation of the pastor. You don't do everything, either in the church or in the world. You aren't a one-man congregation, and you aren't a one-man city. But your work has a universal scope. Through the people you serve and teach and train, you send out the light and life of God into every corner of the city of man. Pastoral ministry is intensively catholic.

This isn't a dream. It's not a vague hope. This is God's plan. The Father sent the Son and Spirit to renew individuals, societies, creation, everything. Through Christ, everything is made new. New creation breaks in.

Prophets see this as a restoration of the garden: When the Spirit is poured out, people are given new hearts of obedience, and the desert blossoms like Eden (Ezek 36). When the Spirit is poured out, the broken city rises from the dust. In the last days, the days of Jesus' reign, the mountain of the house of the Lord rises to be chief of the mountains. The law flows out, the nations stream in, and they learn peace. Lambs and lions lie down together. Children play beside snakes' nests (Isa 11). The nations beat their swords to ploughs and stop making war (Isa 2).

When you form a communion of witnesses, you're carrying out the Lord's catholic program of universal redemption.

Your work is catholic in another sense too. Since the eleventh century, the church has been divided east and west. Since the Reformation, the western church has been divided between Roman Catholics and Protestants. Early on, Protestantism split between German and Swiss varieties and has continued to split into ever-smaller subdivisions since.

We must say it bluntly: This is *not* what Jesus wants for His church. Jesus asked His Father to make His disciples "one," one like the Son is one with the Father and the Father with the Son. The Father is "in" the Son and the Son "in" the Father, and Jesus wants the church to be united in the same fashion. He wants the church to be a visible, human, communal manifestation of the unity of Father and Son. The disciples of Jesus can be one in this way because the Spirit takes us up into the unity of the Father and Son. They are "in us," and we are "in Them" (John 17), and so we may be in each other.

In this prayer, Jesus is simply asking that His Father complete the work He began with Abraham. Even without sin, human beings would have developed in a variety of ways. Some would have settled near the sea and become traders; others would have farmed. Some would have been in cities, some in the country. Cultures and languages would have developed differently.

Sinless Eskimos will still have their umpteen words for snow. Yet the human race would have been at peace, the different languages and cultures in harmony. Without sin, different interests and values would not have led to war.

That's not what happened. When he sinned, Adam was estranged from God. He was also estranged from his wife, and in the next generation one of his sons murdered the other. Ten generations later, the world was so filled with violence that God ended it all with the flood. Even after the flood, human beings rebelled. At Babel, they attempted to unite the human race, but in defiance of God. In response, God scattered them, confusing their languages. The linguistic, cultural, and religious diversity of our world is touched by the sin of Adam and Babel. Whatever legitimate diversity there is sours into hatred and bloodshed.

After Babel, God didn't wipe the world clean as He had done in the flood. Instead, He determined to renew the world from within. He called Abraham and promised that in his seed all the nations of the earth would be blessed. They would remain different. They would retain their cultural customs and linguistic habits. But they would all be brought under the blessing of God. And they would live in harmony. This promise to Abraham is the source of the prophetic visions of global peace.

Jesus is the seed of Abraham, the one in whom this promise, like all promises, is fulfilled. Jesus broke down the dividing wall between Jew and Gentile. In Him there is no Jew or Gentile. At Pentecost, the Spirit provided the antidote to Babel. The Spirit makes it possible for the gospel to be understood in every one of the confused tongues of Babel. The Spirit didn't erase linguistic differences. He harmonized those differences. Gathered by the Spirit, the body of Christ consists of people from every tribe, tongue, nation, and people. The church is the new human race, a diverse yet harmonious city.

Or, she *should* be.

Not all church divisions are wrong. Sometimes, churches become synagogues of Satan, and true believers need to flee. Sometimes, churches switch sides and begin to persecute the faithful. The Harlot who drinks martyr blood is a false *church* (Rev 17).

Not all church conflicts are wrong. Conflicts are unavoidable, and often good. Sometimes the gospel is under attack, and pastors especially must defend it. Sometimes heretics and unbelievers take charge, and the faithful need to fight. Until the new Jerusalem is consummated as a new heavens and new earth, the church will know war.

This isn't unfortunate. It's one of the fields of Jesus' holy war. It's one of the privileges of being with Jesus: We get to fight alongside Him. Some divisions are the result of our stage in history—the fact that we haven't crossed the finish line yet. The city is still under construction, still descending from heaven.

Yet when we're honest, we realize that many of the church's conflicts are not like this. Many of them are manifestations of pride, lust for power, jockeying for prestige or fame. Often the church divides because she follows the national, cultural, and tribal divisions of the world. American Christians support American wars against European Christians. The Pentecostal church, called to be a city of peace and harmony, mirrors Babel. The Bride stops listening to the Bridegroom and gets seduced by a serpent. For centuries, many Christians have refused to seek or preserve unity. For centuries, the church has betrayed herself and her Lord.

Pastor Theo, you're called to work in whatever ways you can to overcome these divisions and pursue unity in the church. That means at least this: You should have a "catholic" understanding of the church. That means you should recognize that the church is universal and all congregations are part of the same global communion.

Practically, it means you should receive all other believers from every church at the Lord's table. The table belongs to Jesus, and the church has no right to exclude someone whom Jesus accepts. Catholics, Orthodox, Protestants, Pentecostals, and every other coloration of Christian should be at the same table as the one Bride of the one Husband.

It also means this: Don't receive anyone as a member of your church who has been disciplined by another church. The other church may be wrong; they may be a cult. But don't take anyone's say-so. Check with the previous church. Honor other pastors as servants of Christ.

But this pursuit of catholicity can take many other forms. Get to know the other pastors in your neighborhood or town. Visit them, talk to them, listen to them, pray for and with them. Ask them for prayer requests, and pray for their needs during public worship. Look for opportunities to worship and serve together. Have an annual communion meal together with as many churches as you can get.

Most towns in the U.S. have pastors' associations where pastors from various churches meet regularly for a meal and fellowship, perhaps for prayer. That's a wonderful thing and a sign of the unity of the church.

But it's only a beginning. Together, the pastors of the churches are the guardians of the city. They are the "angels" at the gates of new Jerusalem (Rev 2-3), messengers and spokesmen for God. And pastors are guardians of the city of man in which they minister. Pray together to discover ways to fulfill this vocation. Invite city leaders to visit the pastors' association. Visit the mayor and ask him what the city needs. Visit the police chief, the fire chief, the city attorney, the city controller. Pray for them, pastor them.

You represent God's city within the city, and you lead the urban renewal project that is the church's mission. Be alert to the city's needs—food deserts, high crime, gang violence, poverty and unemployment. Pray and plan with other pastors about how the churches can help to address these needs.

Jesus wants His church to be united. He also wants His church to be pure. We aren't allowed to choose one over the other. We're called to seek unity in truth, as well as the truth of unity. Fighting heresy and false teaching is part of unifying the church because false teaching and idolatry are the fundamental sources of division.

The pursuit of unity is disruptive in itself. Don't think that you can pursue unity without riling up other Christians. Denominational traditions become so engrained that churches view any deviation as apostasy. It becomes nearly impossible to admit that my tradition might have gotten some things wrong or that I have something to learn from Christians outside my church. If you're a Protestant pastor and you start fraternizing with Catholic or Orthodox priests, expect other Protestants to protest.

Don't let the protests deter you. Fight for the truth. Fight for unity. Fight opponents of unity with as much vigor as you fight enemies of truth.

The rewards are great. As the church expresses her unity, she becomes a real alternative to the fractured, polarized city of man. As the church acts on this unity, she brings out the leaves of the tree of life, which are for the healing of the nations. As you fulfill your role as a catholic pastor, you are an angel at the gate.

To Pastor Theo

Pastoral ministry is a demanding job. It's a big job, than which none is bigger. It's not for the lazy or time-servers. It's not a calling for cowards. It requires all the fruits of the Spirit— passionate, relentless love, love that is patient, humble, courageous, cunning.

But it has rewards. These rewards rarely take the form of fame and fortune. Instead, pastoral ministry comes with the reward of sharing in the ministry of Jesus by the Spirit. Sharing Jesus' ministry means the privilege to suffer shame for His name (Acts 5:41). It comes with the reward of sharing in Jesus' grand construction project, His work of transforming the cities of men into the city of God. In that work, Pastor Theo, you are a foreman. Get to work.

But there might be a hitch. Perhaps this vision of pastoral ministry inspires you. Maybe you want to have weekly Eucharist, but you can't persuade your elders or the people even to use the word "Eucharist." Perhaps you want to pursue local unity among the churches but fear reprisals from other pastors in your denomination.

Real life can be frustrating to reformers. Don't give in to frustration. Minister to the people in front of you. Serve their needs. Teach, correct, disciple, pray for them. Lead them into the Lord's presence in worship. Plant seeds of renewal in the church, and wait for the Spirit to water and grow them. Even if the church isn't all you hope for, even if the church appears embarrassingly feeble, so long as you are faithful, you're building God's city.

Jesus is the Lord of His church and will guide it as He pleases. Trust Him, and be patient.

5 TREASURES OF KINGS

The nations shall walk by its light,
and the kings of the earth shall bring their glory into it. . . .
And the leaves of the tree [of life]
were for the healing of the nations.
Revelation 21:24; 22:2

There are Theos who are pastors. There are many more Theos and Theas who *aren't* pastors. With such a stress on the role of the pastor in chapter 4, does the Theopolitan vision have anything left for the non-pastor? Is the Theopolitan vision a latter-day form of clericalism?

Not at all. The church is a visible community of real-life men and women and children with real bodies and souls. It's a city among the cities of men. John's vision makes it clear that new Jerusalem is the whole people of God. The gates are named for people—the twelve tribes of Israel (Rev 21:12). The foundation stones are named for people—the twelve apostles (21:14). From Peter (1 Pet 2:9-10), we know that the church's walls are made from living stones—people, church members.

That's implicit in the materials that make up the foundation stones. The foundations of Jerusalem are precious gems, twelve of them (21:19-20). In the Mosaic system, the priest wore a breast-plate with twelve gems, each of which was engraved with a name of a tribe of Israel (Exod 29). New Jerusalem is a Bride dressed like a priest, and her gemstones, like the priest's, represent people.

Throughout Scripture, the houses of God represent the people of God. The tabernacle was modeled after the garden of Eden and Mount Sinai. It was also an architectural representation of the people of God. When Nebuchadnezzar took Judah into exile, the temple, its furnishings, and its liturgical tools went into exile too (cf. 2 Kgs 25). Those furnishings and tools represented the people of Israel devoted to Yahweh's service.

I've assumed throughout this book that new Jerusalem in all its details is a description of people. It's a liturgical city where the people of God gather. It's a city of light because the Word is preached there. The water that flows through and out of the city is the Spirit, who carries men and women from the city into their mission in the world.

So the Theopolitan vision isn't a vision of *pastoral* ministry alone. It's a vision of the church in the world and of the church's mission in and to the world. It's a vision of the church, the *whole* church, as God's heavenly city on earth.

As a city, the church has an order. That order is inherent in the church, not some add-on pasted on the outer wall. The order has a hierarchical aspect: Some are leaders, most are not. That hierarchy is inherent in the church, not some "visible" accident on an invisibly egalitarian substance. The church is a city, God's city, God's future city in the present, and cities are organized communities with responsibility and authority distributed in unequal measure.

That doesn't exclude "lay" men and women any more than stressing the need for good political leadership rules out the role of citizens. The two are necessary to one another, mutually defining. Without shepherds, the flock wanders, but without a flock, what's the use of a shepherd?

Besides, the hierarchy of the church is a complex, mobile hierarchy. There are leaders, but the leaders lead a community of the gifted. *Every* member shares the same Spirit that equips the leaders to lead wisely and well. *Every* member receives gifts from the Spirit that are necessary for edifying, building up, the body of Christ. Each member is an organ of the body that serves the needs of the entire body. A member may see, hear, smell, handle, walk, or speak, but he or she does it for the sake of the whole body.

A pastor is a spokesman in the church, the mouth of the body of Christ. With respect to public, liturgical speech, there's a hierarchy with the pastor at the peak of the pyramid. Yet the pastor's speech is hardly the only speech in the church. His speech is priestly speech, speech that establishes foundations; it's angelic speech that guards gates. But within those gates, people speak in prayer, praise, teaching, correction, rebuke, encouragement, sympathy. In many situations, the pastor's speech isn't at the peak. Often, the pastor *listens*.

To speak effectively, the pastor relies on other organs. If the church is going to be more than talk, it needs to be more than a big mouth. It needs hands to serve, feet to go, chests to fight. When we think of the church as a teaching body (which it is), the pastor may be seen as the honcho. When we think of the church as a ministry of mercy (which it is), the women in the soup kitchen take the lead. When we think of the church as a house of prayer (which it is), the old lady in her prayer chair is chief.

This isn't an egalitarian community of interchangeable parts. It's a body of many members, with a complex, oscillating hierarchy that depends on the activity and perspective.

All that is to say that you, non-pastor Theos and Theas, are as essential to the church as your brothers who are pastors. You are essential to the liturgical work of the church. *You* are the body, called by Jesus and equipped by His Spirit, to build yourself up into the full stature of Christ. *You* are the army deployed to bring the kingdoms of the world into the kingdom of Christ, to bring the treasures of Havilah into the Edenic city. *You* are the water flowing from the sanctuary to refresh the land; your works are the light shining out to the nations so that the kings of the earth bring their treasures.

Pretty picture. But how does that actually work?

We can start to answer that question by recalling that the church, like Israel, is a kingdom of priests, a royal priesthood (1 Pet 2:9-10). What might that mean?

Priestly People

In the old covenant, priesthood was limited to the descendants of Aaron and later restricted to the clan of Zadok among the descendants of Aaron. Qualification for priesthood was, the writer to the Hebrews says, "fleshly" (Heb 7), which is to say, genealogical.

Jesus is the new High Priest, but of a different order. He's a priest after the order of Melchizedek, a priest greater than Abraham and therefore greater than Aaron, who descended from Abraham. Judged by flesh, Jesus doesn't qualify for priesthood. He's qualified differently. He's priest by the "power of an indestructible life," priest by resurrection (Heb 7:16).

Jesus alters the form of priesthood. When there's a change of priesthood, there's also a change of law (Heb 7:12). Specifically, the law that changes is the law that governs inclusion in the priesthood. Jesus shatters that law by becoming a priest differently. But He doesn't just shatter it only for Himself. He shatters it for the people of God. From Jesus' resurrection onward, priests are no longer qualified by genealogy. A man doesn't become a priest by physical descent from a priest, nor even by a success of ordination. In the new covenant, a priest becomes a priest by resurrection, by baptismal incorporation into the resurrection of Christ.

That's what Luther said: All of the baptized are priests. Men and women and children are ordained into the Christian priesthood by passing through the waters of baptism. They are all, in Thomas Aquinas's terminology, "deputed" (I prefer to translate it as "deputized") to a role in the Christian liturgy. Within the company of the baptized, some men are further designated as pastors to lead the liturgy and guard the gates. Pastors are priests leading a communion of priests. But the pastor is no more a priest than the lowest member.

If we're all priests, then the liturgy—the priestly service—is an act of the entire congregation. In the medieval Catholic Church, the congregation passively watched as the priests performed the Mass in a strange language. That still happens in some traditions today. That isn't how Christian worship is supposed to work. It's not a biblical model of worship. The liturgy is the work of the *people*, the whole people, each in his or her different capacity.

That means: Every member of the church draws near to the courts of the Lord in song and accepts the Lord's invitation to enter His house. Every member confesses sin and believes the pastor's declaration of forgiveness. Every member ascends in song into heavenly places. Every member prays. Every member hears the reading and preaching of the word. Every member shares the bread and cup, and every member receives the good word, as the name of God is pronounced over and placed on them.

This all sounds very formal, perhaps even formalistic. It sounds dead. It isn't. In the liturgy, Christians enter into the most intimate communion with God, together. We hear and eat and drink Jesus, so that we are His and He is ours, so that He is in us as we are in Him. The liturgy is the place and time when heaven and earth meet, when we are caught up to heavenly places to join the angels and saints in their joyful assembly (Heb 12:18-24). It's the time when the Spirit descends to hover over the earth to form it afresh.

In the liturgy, we anticipate the ultimate future of humanity and of the universe. Someday, all creation will be gathered before the throne in praise. Someday, the human race will sing to the Lamb in an eternal city. Someday, we will celebrate the marriage supper of the Lamb, when our Husband will rejoice over us with exultation and speak to us with words of grace.

That someday comes every Sunday. The liturgy isn't just a picture of what will be. It's a *foretaste* of what will be. It's not merely a glimpse of the city to come. It *is* the city to come, present in the present, the coming city come among us. If you're baptized into the Christian priesthood, you have an essential role anticipating new Jerusalem. If you're a member of the body, you *are* the coming city.

New Jerusalem wouldn't exist without you. Without you, there'd be no sanctuary-city whose breadth, length, and height are the same. Without you, there'd be no city where the light of the word is spoken, believed, done. Without you, there'd be no life in the city, only an empty plaza with very, very high walls.

Pastors should organize the service to maximize congregational participation. Liturgy is active, vigorous, a spoken or, better, a sung dialogue between pastor and people, between Christ's representative and the Bride. There's a role for choirs but, as a rule, the congregation shouldn't sit watching and listening, as if the liturgy were a clerical concern. The congregation should confess faith together, pray together, say the "Amen" together. The liturgy should include common prayers—collects spoken by the whole congregation, the Lord's prayer, litanies in which the congregation responds to the minister's calls to prayer.

Some churches try to correct congregational passivity by giving various people in the congregation a leadership role in worship. One member reads the Scripture, another prays, another sings a solo. That's a liturgical mistake, in two ways.

It's a mistake because the pastor is ordained for the specific purpose of leading the liturgy. That's his job and should no more be delegated to others than a quarterback should delegate his role to the left tackle (which he may do—but only for a trick play).

It's a mistake also because it assumes that liturgical leadership is the only form of liturgical participation. Members don't need to take over leadership to participate. In a biblically organized liturgy, the people are never simply watching the minister do the liturgy. *They* do the liturgy along with the minister, precisely in their role as the people. They are active in worship by being the congregation.

To do the liturgy well, members should prepare. Families can sing hymns and Psalms in their homes. The church's leaders might organize evenings of Psalm-singing to teach the congregation to sing better and to teach new Psalms and hymns. Parents should teach their children prayers and creeds. Members might want to read the upcoming sermon texts ahead of time and reflect on them afterward.

We're idolaters, and the liturgy doesn't come naturally. We need training, and the family is one place where we can be trained. Family worship isn't the same as congregational worship, but it can be boot camp for congregational worship.

Some of you Theos and Theas might be inspired by the Theopolitan vision but find yourselves in churches that are indifferent or hostile. You want the church to sing Psalms, but the pastor and congregation prefer sappy but familiar hymns. You want weekly communion, but the pastor is worried it will become rote. You're looking for a church where the congregation is vigorously active in the worship, but every church has a praise band that performs before a passive congregation.

What should you do? If the church is faithful to the gospel, start by giving thanks for the congregation, pastor, and church you already attend. Thank God for their faithfulness, for their ministries and evangelism, for the truth that is communicated.

Thankfulness isn't complacency. You can give thanks and also criticize and offer suggestions. But without thankfulness, even legitimate criticisms and suggestions will arise from an ungodly, embittered spirit. If you can't find anything to give thanks for, you shouldn't be there. If the church has betrayed the gospel, protest. If the protest fails, leave.

When you do criticize, do it directly to the church's leaders. Don't start talking to other members to form a sub-congregation of complaint, what Pastor Douglas Wilson calls a "fellowship of the grievance." Grievance is a powerful force for forming bonds, but the bonds are demonic. Whatever criticisms or suggestions you offer to the pastor or other leaders, remember that they are your shepherds who are charged by Jesus to keep watch for your soul (Heb 13:17).

Remember that you are called to obey them and honor them (Heb 13:17). You don't have to agree with them. But you *must* honor them as Christ's appointed shepherds. Appeal, don't demand. Suggest, don't give orders. And pray that the Lord will lead the leaders into a deeper appreciation of biblical worship. And remember that, however feeble the church seems, it is contributing to the work of building God's city. However pathetic, it *is* the city of the living God, heaven sent to earth.

Building the Body

We were talking about being priests. Priestly work is liturgical work. But priests do other things besides worship.

Guarding was one of the chief duties of Levites and priests. They stood armed at the doorways of the tabernacle and temple to prevent unauthorized intruders (Num 1:53; 3:10).

That role was essential to Israel's health and safety. If the Lord's house became defiled, He wouldn't stay. Ezekiel took a tour of Solomon's temple, which had become as filled with idols and images as an Egyptian temple. No wonder that was followed by a vision of Yahweh's glory leaving the temple (Ezekiel 8—11). Yahweh is holy, and He doesn't stay in an unholy house.

The prospect of the Lord's departure was a terror to Israel. Yahweh was their shield, their mighty man, their king. Without Him, they were easy prey for the larger and more militant nations around them. Without Him, they were doomed to lose their king, their temple, their land. Without Yahweh and His Name in the temple, Israel wasn't Israel.

If you're baptized, then you're a priestly guardian of the new house of God, the temple of the Spirit that is the church. Your pastor or pastors have a special responsibility to guard the house, since they're the angels at the gates. But you can't leave it to the pastors to guard the purity of the house alone. *You* are responsible to keep the holy house holy.

If a brother sins against you, confront and correct him, involving other church members if necessary (Matt 18:15-20). If a sister is drifting away, you're equipped with the Spirit to restore her with gentle humility (Gal 6:1). If you know that a member of the church is developing an evil spirit of bitterness and ingratitude, drifting into unbelief, don't wait around for the pastor to notice. *You're* supposed to intervene (Heb 3:12).

In a healthy congregation, most of the pastoral care and correction isn't carried out by the pastor. It's carried out by members, as they "one-another one another," exhorting, encouraging, confronting, correcting, loving. The church has a pastor-police force, but they're chief policemen of a *self*-policing community.

That's hard work. It's not easy to confront someone else with his or her sin. You'd rather avoid it, and you may even be tempted to excuse your inaction with a pious gloss:

"I'm covering it with love," you tell yourself. Sometimes, that's the right thing to do. Often, it's an evasion. Christians need to confront far more than they do. We need to learn what it means to be our brothers' keepers.

You do this for the same reason that the priests and Levites guarded the temple. If idolatry takes root in the church, if the church drifts into lukewarmness and lethargy, if the church begins to follow false teachers or shrinks back from courageous witness—then Jesus will remove the candlestick (cf. Rev 2—3). The Spirit abandoned Saul when he persisted in rebellion (1 Sam 16:14). The Spirit abandoned the temple when Israel worshiped idols (Ezek 8—11). The Spirit will withdraw from a believer or a church that becomes infested with idolatry, unrepented sin, impurities (Eph 4:30; 1 Thes 5:19). We're called to weed the garden and fight off the serpents so that we don't get expelled.

First and foremost, we're responsible for *ourselves*. Each of us is a temple of the Spirit, called to guard the doors of our hearts so that we don't grieve or quench the Spirit. We guard our eyes, ears, hands, feet from whatever might defile us. We're careful about what we see and hear, what our hands do, where our feet take us.

When we do sin and need cleansing, we confess: "If we confess our sins, God who is faithful and just will forgive our sins and cleanse us from all unrighteousness" (1 John 1:9-10). The church shouldn't be a place where sin hides and festers. Like a poisonous fungus, sin grows deadly in the dark. It dies when it's brought to light. We bring our own sins to light in confession. That's one of the main ways we guard the holy city of God.

Take the log out of your eye first, Jesus says. He doesn't say we should ignore the speck in our brother's eye. We remove the log from our own eye so we can see clearly to help our brother with his minor vision problem.

This sounds defensive, negative. That's partly true. A guard has a defensive role. But the new covenant brings something new, something more aggressive and positive.

Under the old covenant, death spread. Touch a woman during her menstrual period, and you're defiled. Sit where she sat, and you're defiled. If she touches you, you're defiled. Same with a man who has a polluting flow from his genitals (Lev 15). To avoid impurity, Jews avoided lepers, menstruants, other impure persons, or washed themselves constantly to get rid of the stain.

Not Jesus. A woman with a flow of blood touches Jesus, and Jesus remains clean and the woman is healed (Mark 5:25-34). Jesus touches dead bodies and remains clean. The dead rise (John 11). Jesus enters a world of spreading death and arrests its spread. Death stops here, with Jesus.

Then Jesus throws death into reverse. The life of the Spirit spreads from Jesus to lepers, to women, to the dead, to us. Then, in Acts, the Spirit equips the apostles to do the same. Like Jesus (and Elijah and Elisha before Him), the apostles raise dead bodies (Acts 9:36-39; 20:7-12). Because the life-Spirit of Jesus dwells in them, they aren't defiled, but overcome defilement.

We must still guard ourselves from the defilement of lies, lust, anger, all the things that come out of our hearts but are encouraged by what goes into our eyes and ears (Matt 15:10-11). But we're filled with the same Spirit that filled Jesus. We're clothed with the Spirit of life, and we're His agents for the conquest of death. We guard, but we don't cower in fear. We guard in hope, confident of our victory. We enter the realm of death and defilement to bring life and health.

Guarding is one of the chief responsibilities of the Christian priesthood. But it's not the only one. Christian priests are also teachers. Not all members of the church have the gifts and training to teach officially. But every member has some teaching role.

If you are a parent, God requires you to teach His word to His children (Deut 6; Prov 1; Eph 6:1-4), to train them to mature as disciples of Jesus. If you're a single adult, you're called to teach your friends and family members as opportunity arises. If you learn that one of your friends is going off the rails, doubting basic biblical teaching, you're called to teach correctively. When another member suffers, you teach by reminding them of the Lord's faithfulness. You teach by your faithful, Christlike co-presence in the heart of their pain.

Every member is a witness, called to teach unbelieving friends, family members, co-workers, as opportunities arise. Even children teach one another. Nearly every Christian parent has heard one of his or her exhortations repeated by one child to another: "You shouldn't do that. Jesus doesn't like that."

Priests alone entered the holy place to offer incense at the golden altar (Lev 24), the incense that represented the ascending prayers of the saints (Ps 141:2). Even in the old covenant, the priestly nation could pray anywhere at any time. After Solomon built the temple, their prayers were directed toward the house (1 Kgs 8), where the Lord promised to put His eyes and ears. The temple was an exchange point between earthly Israel and their heavenly Lord. As they prayed toward the house, the Lord heard and answered from heaven.

We no longer pray toward an architectural temple in a particular location on earth. We have a human temple, the incarnate Name. In the new covenant, the Son of God has taken on human eyes and ears so that He can hear when we pray "in His Name."

Prayer is one of the chief ways we one-another one another. We bring all the little needs and annoyances of life to God in prayer. We cast our anxieties, and the anxieties of our brothers and sisters, on the Lord.

As a former pastor of mine used to say, biblical prayers usually have a "so that" clause, and the "so that" is crucial. "Heal Aunt Agatha," we pray. . . . but *why*? Why do we want Agatha back on her feet? We need a "so that": "Heal Aunt Agatha so she can get back to teaching Sunday School, or volunteering at the soup kitchen, or serving Christ as an executive of a multi-national corporation." Prayers for the little needs are prayers for the extension of the ministry of the church. Even the smallest prayer is ultimately about building the heavenly city that renews the cities of men.

Our prayers should reach as far as God's promises. He promises to save us from the guilt and penalty of sin, yes. We should pray for that, for ourselves, our families, friends, neighbors. But He also promises to make the kingdoms of this world the kingdom of the Lord and of His Christ (Rev 11:15). He promises that kingdom will grow from a stone into a mountain that fills the earth (Dan 2). He promises that the kingdom that started as small as a mustard seed will become a tree where the birds nest (Matt 13). He promises that the earth will be filled with the knowledge of the Lord as the waters cover the sea (Isa 11:9).

He promises that Jesus will reign until all His enemies are placed beneath His feet (1 Cor 15:25). He promises to break the teeth of oppressors (Ps 58:6), to install His Son as king to quiet the raging nations (Ps 2), to establish justice and peace among nations (Ps 72; Is 9), to raise up good kings who will be nursing fathers to His church (Isa 60:10-22). To be faithful in prayer, make your prayers political.

Tune your prayers to His promises, and so participate in His work of global redemption.

The Liturgy After the Liturgy

In case you haven't noticed, let me alert you to a pattern: What you do in the liturgy is what you do, in a different mode and key, outside the liturgy.

In the liturgy, the pastor comforts and rebukes and shepherds you by word; so you should do the same within the body. In the liturgy, you confess and intercede; and that sets the pattern for a life of prayer. In the liturgy, you receive the Lord's hospitality at His table. And He commands you, "Go and do likewise." The heavenly city is a sanctuary city, its entire civic life a liturgy. The gathered liturgy of the Lord's day sets the pattern for the dispersed liturgy of day-to-day life.

Jesus spends a lot of His ministry at table, and He uses the table as a model of discipleship (Luke 14). How do you behave at the table? Do you jockey for position? Do you want to sit near the coolest and most important people? Or do you take the lowest seat? Whom do you invite to your table? Important people, who will return the invitation and help you climb the social ladder? Or do you invite the lame, blind, outcasts from the highways and byways?

The answer to these questions should be determined by the answer to this question: How does *Jesus* conduct Himself at table? Whom does *He* invite?

God's hospitality forms the one body. Our hospitality to one another builds the body. Our tables extend Eucharist, filling our lives with festive thanksgiving. The Father gives His Son in the Spirit at His table. At our table, we share the good gifts of God with one another, extending the gifts that God has given at His table. At His table, God gives honor to those who lack honor, and we should do the same at our tables. Our tables are opportunities to extend the joy, life, and gratitude of the liturgy into everyday life. The table is the main biblical model of charity—not a self-negating gift but a sharing and exchange and mutual enjoyment of goods.

In all these ways, and more, the liturgy extends into a liturgy of body life, a liturgy that builds the body.

When we recognize this dynamic, debates about ordination take on a different color. Today, churches are deeply divided over the question of women's ordination. We at Theopolis believe that only men should be ordained. But that is *far* from saying that only men have a role in the work of the church. Every member—man, woman, child—is responsible to guard and build the body. Every member has a place in the liturgy, both on the Lord's day and during the week.

The big event of the church's life is the liturgy, but the liturgy is the work of the *whole* people. The minister leads, but he leads the congregation in a corporate act. And apart from the liturgy, *most* of the work of the church *isn't* done by the pastors. Most of it is done by men and women and children who edify the body in myriads of ways.

"All well and good," you might say. "But I could find something similar in other manuals of church life. How does this differ from other agendas for church community? How is this a *Theopolitan* vision?" Good question. It's a question I asked myself, as you can see from the fact that I wrote the question down a couple of sentences back.

Remember chapter 1? There I pointed out that the New Testament describes the church in political terms, as an outpost of the city that is to come, as the *ekklesia*, the assembly of a new city, a new assembly that determines the health and future of the cities of men where it takes root. All the aspects of "body life" that I've been describing are dimensions of the "civic life" of the church. These are some of the ways that the church exists, grows, and matures as the city of God within the cities of men. These are some of the ways the church becomes a counter-city that disrupts, provokes, and challenges the civic pathologies that surround it.

Your church may not look much like a city. You don't all live in the same part of town. You don't have a roads department or a fire department or a police department. You can't tax or issue business licenses. Your church might seem more a parasite on the city than a city. You drive to church using roads that the city maintains. Your church building had to meet local building and zoning codes. Your pastor calls you using a cell phone network that doesn't belong to the church. Your church may look less like a city than like another sub-group within the city.

That's all true. The church doesn't have *all* the features of a city, whether ancient or modern. But the Bible still describes it as a city, and we need to think through what that means. In what ways is the church city-like?

For starters, your church has geographic limits. Even if the members of your church live forty miles apart at opposite ends of a metropolis, you occupy roughly the same space on the planet. You have a common way of life and loyalty to one another. Your church has leaders, budgets, buildings, organization, holidays and celebrations. The church reflects the variety of the human race—old and young, men and women, people from various tribes and tongues and nations—like a cosmopolitan city.

Every city has a distinctive way of life. Every city has an ethos. New Yorkers are bustling, Bostonians are rude, Londoners are cool, and residents of Birmingham, Alabama, have an inferiority complex toward Atlanta. Every city has particular practices, whether it's a port city, a political center, a tourist destination.

The church is a civic community because it has a distinct ethos and a distinct way of life. How? Let me suggest some specific ways.

- Every week, Christians assemble to worship. We honor Jesus as Lord and King. These are *public* truths. Jesus isn't "my personal Savior and Lord" the way my fitness coach (if I had one) is "my personal trainer." Jesus is Lord of all. He is King of kings. In every worship service, we acknowledge and rejoice in His kingship. Every worship service, we declare our loyalty to another king and another kingdom, a city that has come and will come. In every worship service, we remind the leaders of the city of man that they are subjects of the High King. We remind the world and ourselves that our final loyalty isn't to the nation, people, or city of our natural birth but the new city of the baptized.

- The early church was unique in its sexual ethics. Romans held marriage and family in high esteem, but their conception of family was quite different from Christians'. Roman men had mistresses, visited prostitutes, had free rein to take sexual advantage of male or female slaves. Roman women accepted the men's license and the double standard. Christians condemned all extra-marital sexual activity as unholy, for men as much as for women. And they policed the sexual activity of members. Paul commanded the Corinthians to expel a man who was committing incest (1 Cor 6). Still today, in our "enlightened" age, the church is called to teach and live by a biblical sexual ethic. That alone sets apart the church radically from most of the cities in which she dwells.

- Christian priests teach, and Christian parents teach children. If you're called to train them as disciples, then you're going to have to reject alternative training that would deform them as un-disciples. You're called to provide a Christian *paideia*, not the statist *paideia* of liberal democracy. Yes, I'm saying you should get your kids out of public schools. Do it now. Don't let your children—the children of *Jesus*—be discipled as unbelievers. Taking our responsibility to disciple our children seriously will make us a very different sort of people from the cities in which we live. Over generations, those who are discipled under the pedagogy of the church will live in a different moral and intellectual and cultural universe than citizens of the cities of men. This is what is happening in the U.S. as graduates of home school and Christian schools come to adulthood.

These are aspects of the liturgy after the liturgy, the liturgy that is the way of life of the city of God.

As I've stressed throughout, being God's city among the cities of men comes with a cost. The city of man has its own liturgies—liturgies of consumerist commerce, liturgies of sexual freedom, liturgies of messianic politics (can you say "Trump rally"?). The church doesn't play out her liturgy in a liturgy-free environment. She enacts God's liturgy to confront the liturgies of men.

The liturgies of the human city encourage unchecked consumerism, insatiable desire for goods, 24/7 consumption; the liturgy of the city of God is a liturgy of thankfulness and contentment. The liturgies of the human city celebrate nearly infinite sexual freedom and treat Christian sexual ethics as repressive; the liturgy of the city of God is a liturgy of chastity, marital faithfulness, union in sexual difference. The liturgy of the human city places hope in the next Great Leader; the liturgy of the city of God confesses *one* Lord, Jesus the Christ. We enact the Christian liturgy for the sake of the cities of men so that their cultural liturgies are dismantled and transformed, so that their civic habits and values conform to the word of the King whom we worship.

When we really live out the liturgy after the liturgy, we're bound to clash with the city of man. We're bound to have opportunities for some form of martyrdom.

The Church Is Mission

Every Christian is a priest with a liturgical vocation. Every Christian participates in the public work of the liturgy. Every Christian is gifted by the Spirit to build up the body of Christ, to extend the truth-telling, word, and table of the liturgy into the everyday life of the church. Every Christian participates in "reasonable service," the liturgy of body life (Rom 12).

Every Christian is also a missionary, a participant in the mission of the church. Among Evangelicals, this is a truism, but it's understood reductively if mission is reduced to personal evangelism.

We *should* take every opportunity that arises to speak the good news to people who do not know Jesus. Churches need to train members to do declare the gospel, and individual church members should participate in evangelism efforts.

But if the gospel is inherently political, if God's polis is inherent in the gospel, evangelism will look quite different. Gospel presentations like those found in old tracts, or used in older evangelism programs like the Four Spiritual Laws or Evangelism Explosion focus on individual sin, individual conversion, individual faith, individual salvation. The cross of Jesus is a bridge to bring us across the chasm back to God. Jesus is the answer to the question, "Why should I let you into my heaven?"

Those kinds of presentations have their place, but they miss the political and cosmic scope of the gospel. The good news is that Jesus is installed as king. It's not merely a message of individual salvation. It's a message of cosmic salvation. The evangelistic invitation is a call to corporate as well as individual repentance.

We might write an evangelism tract along these lines: "Jesus the Son of God is the world's true King. He's King over *you* too. If you don't honor Him as King, you're a rebel, and He punishes rebels. If you want to live now and forever, you'd better get on His good side. You'd better turn from your sins and be loyal to Him."

The end game of evangelism should be membership in the Eucharistic community. The evangelist doesn't aim to get someone to pray a sinner's prayer (perfectly good in itself) or to confess Christ (necessary in itself). Like the apostles on the day of Pentecost, the evangelist urges penitent sinners to be baptized to receive the Holy Spirit (Acts 2). Evangelism is an invitation to a wedding feast (Matt 21), the wedding feast that is the kingdom coming, the wedding feast that is already now at the center of the life of the city of God.

The evangelist urges unbelievers to leave the world, the city of man, and to become citizens of God's city, with its vocation of worship and edification and mission. Evangelism is recruitment of new evangelists. Missionary work aims to expand the number of workers in the mission. We preach the gospel so that others will be caught up by the Spirit in Jesus' work of blessing the nations.

Such an understanding of the gospel greatly expands opportunities for evangelism. You don't need to steer a conversation, awkwardly and unnaturally, toward "spiritual things." Every single conversation has to do with something Jesus claims as His own. As Abraham Kuyper said, "There's not one square inch of creation of which Jesus does not say, 'It is mine.'"

A conversation about the weather is a conversation about the Lord of wind and rain. A conversation about child-rearing or marriage is a conversation about the God who loves His Bride and His children. A conversation about political corruption is a conversation about the God who is Just, the God who intends to establish justice on earth. A conversation about yard work is a conversation about Adam's first calling. A conversation about social media is a conversation about the nature of true community. A conversation about fashion is a conversation about man and woman in the image of God.

If you're filled with awe at the scope of Christ's kingship, if you truly believe that Jesus claims every inch, there's no need to manipulate a conversation toward Jesus. Jesus is always already implicated in everything, for in Him all things cohere.

Even *this* is too narrow a conception of the mission of the church. The church's mission is as broad, as universal, as catholic, as the vocation of humanity. Adam and Eve were created to be fruitful and multiply, to fill the earth, to subdue and rule it (Gen 1:26-28). Men and women exist to carry out this "cultural mandate" to care for the creation and to transform and glorify the creation until the garden becomes a city. God first created earth formless and void, then sculpted it into the ordered and beautiful cosmos we inhabit. As His images, we sculpt the already glorious creation so that it matures from glory to glory.

After Adam sinned, the human race was derailed from that vocation. Human beings continued to fill, subdue, and rule creation, but they filled the earth with violent idolaters, laid waste to the world, abused their brothers and sisters. Jesus comes as Last Adam to put us back on track, to reorient the cultural work of sinners toward the original Adamic mandate, to transform this world into something resembling the city that is yet to come.

The church as an institution doesn't directly carry out this mandate. It's not as if engineers, lawyers, farmers, builders, mayors, homemakers, miners, teachers, doctors, and all the rest are on the church's payroll. The church doesn't carry out the Adamic cultural program in that sense. Yet the church *is* the new Adamic humanity, and in our weekday work as much as in our Sunday liturgical work, we're citizens of the heavenly city. On weekdays as much as on Sundays, we seek the transformation of the city of man so that it comes to image the city of God. Even when we move out of the sanctuary, when we move into the marketplace or courthouse, we enact the liturgy outside the liturgy.

Let's try to be concrete:

- God wants His creation beautified. Beautifying creation was a central part of Adam's commission. Every vocation that contributes to the beautification of the city of man is fulfilling the cultural mandate—from city officials who plan parks, to the engineers who design elegant and efficient roads and bridges, to the caretakers who maintain suburban lawns, to the men who pick up garbage. Many who engage in this work don't intend to fulfill the church's mission, but they contribute to the church's mission nonetheless, insofar as they genuinely make the city of man more like the city of God. Christians involved in any of these vocations are *consciously* glorifying

God by glorifying creation, consciously infusing the beauty of the city of God into the city of man. Shining with the light of the Lamb, refreshed by the water and fruit of life, believers bring the life of the Spirit into the work of beautification.

- The cultural mandate isn't only about the relation of human beings to the creation. It's about human beings in relationship with other human beings. Politics and social work are as much a part of the dominion mandate as engineering. Service "industries" contribute to the comfort, health, joy, and prosperity of the ones they serve. They build up the human city as the exercise of spiritual gifts builds up the body of Christ. A farmer cultivates land to produce a crop that will, at the other end of the chain, sustain people he never meets. He loves distant neighbors. A taxi driver serves his passengers, loves them by bringing them safely (if a little rattled) to their destination. An ambulance driver may be crucial to the survival of a heart attack victim. The nurses, doctors, and other personnel who care for the patient at the hospital edify the city. Many carry out these vocations without a thought for Jesus or His city; but they are bringing their treasures into the city in spite of themselves. Christians engage in these vocations with a conscious intent to transform the city of man into something more like the coming heavenly city. Having received the love of Christ, they share the love of Christ in the world.
- Artists fulfill the creation mandate in a direct way. A musician beautifies the air itself. A painter captures an angle of vision on the world, or imagines another world, which enhances the viewer's vision of reality. These art works adorn the city of man and make it more like the gem-encrusted city of God. Again, Christian artists and musicians do their work for the express purpose of glorifying the city so that it becomes more like the heavenly city of John's vision.
- Christians in political office don't cease to be Christians. Christian political leaders should legislate, judge, act in a way that directs the city of man toward the city of God.

They are still citizens of another city, still under the command of king Jesus. In their political actions as in their private lives, they are under the authority of the church and may be disciplined for advocating or enacting ungodly policies.

It's easy to misunderstand the Christian notion of vocation. Sometimes, we think that the world has its own pre-set menu of callings and that Christians are called to slip in quietly and do their calling Christianly.

That scenario is far too peaceful. The city of man is structured to inhibit Christian faithfulness. We can see obvious examples around us: Christian teachers can't pray at the beginning of a class in American public schools or universities. Christian business owners are pressured to conform to contemporary sexual codes. The lure of commercial success encourages Christians to organize their businesses to maximize profit rather than to serve God and neighbor. The world, as Paul says, is under the control of principalities and powers, world systems that are being overthrown by the Sprit of Jesus.

In such a system, Christians can't simply continue business as usual. If we are faithful, we *will* be disruptive. If we are deeply Christian in our callings, we will find opportunity for martyrdom.

What lies on the far side of the disruption? What kind of city of man do we hope for? We will devote future volumes in this series to answering that question in detail, but at base the answer is simple.

The church is the city of God on a mission of urban renewal. Our aim is to make the city of man more like the city of God, more conformed to the pattern of the heavenly city that John saw from the mountain. As the city of God infiltrates the city of man, Jesus will be acknowledged as King of kings, as ruler of all cities on earth. As the city of God shines the light of the Lamb, the rulers of the city of man will become more attentive to the weak and vulnerable, use their coercive power to beat down the ruthless, shape economic life to the ends of justice, welcome strangers and seek peace. The city of man will never become the city of God; it will never replace the church, the heavenly city, or make it superfluous. But the earthly city of man *will* be—and *has* been—remade into an image of the heavenly city.

You Are My Witnesses

In the end, we come back to witness. A Christian journalist who unmasks the truth about an unjust war, or political corruption, is bearing witness. And he may make the city of man a little more like the coming city of truth. A Christian lawyer devoted to seeking justice and truth is bearing witness. A factory worker who works with cheerfulness and gratitude, who looks for ways to love his fellow-workers, is bearing witness. Only bad artists manipulate their work to evangelistic ends, but artistic work is a form of witness nonetheless.

Illumined by the word and table of the liturgy, every form of life, every vocation, can become light. Every form of life can be shaped Christianly.

A form of life shaped Christianly is a form of life shaped cruciformly. You bear a cross. You're called to follow Jesus no matter what, no matter the cost. Even if a journalist risks being fired if he shines light into a dark corner, he still has to speak. If a Christian lawyer is threatened by powerful people for shattering injustice, he must still pursue justice. If a factory worker discovers that his fellow workers are stealing, he shouldn't stay silent, even if he risks a beating in the parking lot.

Christians often treat their work as a means for achieving a comfortable life. We avoid discomfort. We find ways to cut corners and avert our eyes and assimilate so that we don't risk anything. Whatever Christian living is, it's not riskless. It always involves witness, and witness is always potential martyrdom. If you're a pastor, you're a witness, and a trainer of witnesses. You're a martyr called to form a company of martyrs.

Martyrdom isn't defeat. Martyrdom is victory. When believers witness faithfully in their words and work, we shine the light of God to the world. If we suffer, we end up bearing the bond-marks of Jesus before the world. Whether we "succeed" or "fail," we succeed. Win or lose, we win.

This is the story of Revelation. The martyrs under the altar (Rev 6) are joined by 144,000 additional martyrs (Rev 14), and together they ascend above the firmament to join the heavenly choir (Rev 15). That's good for the martyrs. On earth, their blood shakes down Babylon and shatters the firmament dividing heaven and earth. Eventually, martyrs rule in heaven, seated on thrones (Rev 20), and the heavenly city descends to earth through the hole that martyrs make in the firmament. Witnesses win.

Note that martyrs don't win merely because God commends and exalts them. Martyrs win because their witness in blood shatters the systems and structures of the city of man. Martyrs win because we share in Jesus' triumph over the principalities and powers of this world. As we witness faithfully, God tears down so that He can build up; He uproots so that a new garden can be planted. Martyrdom is a *political* success.

As I said earlier, the mission of the church is *intensively* catholic. Pastors encourage church members to find ways to live out their vocation as witness, in conformity with the commands of Jesus. Christians go about their everyday activities as a way of fulfilling the Lord's mission in the world.

The mission of the church is also *extensively* catholic. The church is called to be one body of mutually indwelling persons and communities. All Christians, not just pastors, are called to seek this unity. All Christians are called to pursue catholicity and unity. Every Christian is a catholic Christian.

"Lay" Christians are crucial to the church's growth toward unity. By the nature of their vocation, most pastors spend most of their time with church members—caring for their needs, teaching and preparing to teach, leading worship or preparing to lead worship. Pastors should be involved in mission outside the church, but their primary vocation is to lead the church to be the church.

Non-pastors, though, are out in the marketplace and city squares, interacting with Christians from other churches on a daily basis. The woman at the next desk is Antiochene Orthodox. The real estate agent is a Southern Baptist. The man who does your wife's hair is Methodist.

Most Christians aren't called to engage in "high level" ecumenical discussions, but men and women of the church can help break down barriers of prejudice, suspicion, and hatred. For starters, treat other believers as brothers and sisters. If they're baptized in the Triune name and attend a church that confesses the truth of Scripture as summarized in the Apostles' Creed, they should be treated as fellow Christians. Conversation may reveal that they don't in fact believe any of it, or that they're living in sin. Then, respond the way you should to a wayward brother in your home church: Correct, rebuke, teach.

Being a catholic Christian has significant implications for your political views. I can speak with some knowledge only about the United States, but perhaps it will be relevant to readers in other countries.

Currently, the U.S. appears to be deeply polarized. The vocal leaders of the different political parties are at odds. A talking head on Fox News blames everything on unpatriotic liberals. Flip the channel, and you'll find a talking head on CNN or MSNBC who blames everything on fascist, racist conservatives.

Those elite differences seem to be dividing citizens outside the District of Columbia and far from TV studios. We cannot be sure whether these divisions will last or whether they will deepen into something more dangerous. I suspect that our divisions run deep and that the U.S. has a rocky century ahead of us.

How does a Christian respond to this? It's devilishly easy to choose sides, to become an echo chamber for your favorite talk radio celebrity, to subject yourself to the discipleship of Fox or CNN. As a starting point, you must resist that. *Jesus*, not American conservatism or liberalism, is Lord. Jesus' commands, not the Constitution, are absolute.

Of course, there are issues where one or another side of the political spectrum has it *right*. Conservatives are right to protect unborn babies. But then liberals are right to insist on our duties to care for refugees and immigrants. Neither side of the political spectrum speaks with the authority of Scripture or even the authority of the church. Christians have to learn to evaluate *every* political issue by Scripture—not by the latest deliverances from your favorite pundit.

Christians must learn to evaluate political questions from the viewpoint of the city of God rather than from the viewpoint of the nation or the city of man. Immigration provides an excellent test case.

This is an exceedingly complicated question. My colleague Alastair Roberts asks *some* of the difficult questions that need to be answered:

> 80% of Nigerian doctors want to move to the West; should we welcome immigration that strips a country of its skilled population? Should we encourage immigration to the US from the Middle East when displaced persons can be settled in the region? To what extent should we accommodate radically different cultures, religions, and social values, and to what extent should we expect people to assimilate? What about the ways that immigration has been weaponized to break down historic

Christian cultural norms in Western societies . . . through multiculturalism or used to empower business and elites through offering cheap labor, while pushing indigenous working classes out of their traditional neighborhoods in many parts of the country? What is a reasonable number to admit? To what extent do we have a responsibility to economic immigrants?

Christians cannot address these and the hundreds of other questions about immigration simply as citizens of a particular country. We can't simply ask, "Is this good for our nation?" We have to think these questions through as citizens of another city, asking what the *church's* responsibility is to strangers who show up on our doorstep.

Looking at these questions from the viewpoint of the church highlights some neglected realities: Many immigrants to the U.S. are Christians. Catholic parishes in the U.S. have been revived by the presence of Latin American immigrants, and African immigrants in New York City are planting churches so fast that they don't have enough pastors. In Europe too, some of the fastest-growing churches consist of African immigrants.

If immigrants are "invaders," as some pundits tell us, we need to ask why God is allowing the once-Christian nations of Europe and the U.S. to be invaded. Is this judgment for our cruelty, greed, lust, unbelief, and idolatry?

Working out a politics centered on the church is especially important in international relations. Christians have too often adopted a simple nationalist stance toward other countries: If my country goes to war, I support it, even if my country is killing Christians and bombing churches in another country. When we do that, we're putting the interests and values of the city of man ahead of the interests of the city of God. It's quite literally demonic and must be exorcised.

In international relations as in domestic policy, we should

form our opinions as citizens of God's city.

Immigration and international relations are complex issues, and I don't intend to sort through all the questions here. My point is a more general one: Christians must resist being captured by political ideologies and combat the temptation to think through political issues in terms of the politics of the city of man. We must retrain ourselves to think and act as citizens of another city.

This won't win you any friends. Conservatives will think you're a globalist turncoat. Liberals will think you're a nostalgic localist. But the Christian can neither choose sides nor simply split the difference. Our political calculus includes a factor that Left and Right all but ignore, the central factor of world politics: God's heavenly city.

To Theo and Thea

Whether you're a pastor or not, you're part of the city of God. By the Spirit, you're equipped as a builder. By the Spirit, you're caught up in the mission of Jesus. You're the light that draws the kings of the earth to Jerusalem, leaves of the tree of life that heal the nations, the river of the water of life. It's through your witness that the principalities and powers will be thrown down, the systems of this world broken to pieces, and a new city take shape. It's through you that Jesus carries out His urban renewal mission to transform the kingdoms of this world into the kingdoms of our Lord and His Christ.

EPILOGUE

I love to read. I read everything I can get my mitts on. I'm not so eager to *do*. Doing is hard work. I can't *do* from my recliner.

I hope you enjoyed reading this book. I hope it was inspiring and edifying. I hope that you Theos and Theas are inspired by the breadth, height, depth, the universal scope of the church's mission.

But I don't want you to stop with reading. I want you to do something. I want you to take whatever is good and right in the Theopolitan vision, and do it.

Start where you are. Do what you can. But *do*.

For you Theos who are pastors, re-commit yourself to studying and teaching the word, all of it, in as much depth as you can. Start singing psalms. Nudge your congregation toward weekly communion. Teach your people that they're part of Jesus' mission of urban renewal. Inspire them to see how they're part of the biggest deal there is.

For you Theos and Theas who aren't pastors, throw yourself into the life of your local church. Pray for your pastors and leaders. Pray that they would conform the church's worship more and more to the Bible. Pray that they would see the breadth and scope of their work and of the church's mission. Sign up to participate in the existing ministries of your home church. Look for opportunities for witness. Discover how your labors fit into the Spirit's work of re-creation. Serve, pray, study.

Jesus the Son of the Father builds His city by His Spirit. But He has given us the astonishing task of sharing in that work. All of you have a job to do. Get to work.

FOR FURTHER READING

Church

Jordan, James B. *The Sociology of the Church*. Eugene, OR: Wipf & Stock, 1999.

Leithart, Peter J. *Against Christianity*. Moscow, ID: Canon Press, 2003.

Leithart, Peter J. *The End of Protestantism*. Grand Rapids: Baker, 2016

Liturgy

Jordan, James B. *Theses on Worship*. Niceville, FL: Transfiguration Press, 1998.

Jordan, James B. *The Liturgy Trap*. Niceville, FL: Transfiguration Press, 1998.

Leithart, Peter J. *Daddy, Why Was I Excommunicated?* Niceville, FL: Transfiguration Press, 1992.

Leithart, Peter J. *Blessed Are the Hungry*. Moscow, ID: Canon Press, 2000.

Leithart, Peter J. *The Priesthood of the Plebs*. Eugene, OR: Wipf & Stock, 2003.

Leithart, Peter J. *From Silence to Song*. Moscow, ID: Canon Press, 2003.

Leithart, Peter J. *The Baptized Body*. Moscow, ID: Canon Press, 2007.

Meyers, Jeffery. *The Lord's Service*. Moscow, ID: Canon Press, 2003.

Bible

Jordan, James B. *Through New Eyes*. Eugene, OR: Wipf & Stock, 1999.

Jordan, James B. *Judges: God's War Against Humanism*. Eugene, OR: Wipf & Stock, 1999.

Jordan, James B. *Creation in Six Days*. Moscow, ID: Canon Press, 1999.

Jordan, James B. *Primeval Saints*. Moscow, ID: Canon Press, 2002.

Jordan, James B. *The Handwriting on the Wall*. Atlanta: American Vision, 2007.

Jordan, James B. *The Vindication of Jesus Christ*. Monroe, LA: Athanasius Press, 2009.

Leithart, Peter J. *A House For My Name*. Moscow, ID: Canon Press, 2000.

Leithart, Peter J. *A Son To Me*. Moscow, ID: Canon Press, 2003.

Leithart, Peter J. *The Promise of His Appearing*. Moscow, ID: Canon Press, 2004.

Leithart, Peter J. *1 & 2 Kings*. Grand Rapids: Brazos, 2006.

Leithart, Peter J. *From Behind the Veil*. Moscow, ID: Canon Press, 2009.

Leithart, Peter J. *Deep Exegesis*. Waco, TX: Baylor University Press, 2009.

Leithart, Peter J. *The Four: A Survey of the Gospels*. Moscow, ID: Canon Press, 2010.

Leithart, Peter J. *Delivered from the Elements of the World*. Downers Grove, IL: IVP, 2016.

Leithart, Peter J. *Revelation, 2 volumes*. London: T&T Clark, 2018.

Leithart, Peter J. *1 & 2 Chronicles*. Grand Rapids: Brazos Press, 2019.

Leithart, Peter J. *Matthew, 2 volumes*. Monroe, LA: Athanasius Press, 2018-2019.

Meyers, Jeffery J. *A Table in the Mist*. Monroe, LA: Athanasius Press, 2007.

Sumpter, Toby. *A Son for Glory*. Monroe, LA: Athanasius Press, 2014.

Wilson, Andrew and Robert, Alastair. *Echoes of Exodus*. Crossway, 2018.

Politics and Culture.

Jordan, James B. *Christendom and the Nations*. Monroe, LA: Athanasius Press, 2019.

Leithart, Peter J. *Brightest Heaven of Invention*. Moscow, ID: Canon Press, 1996.

Leithart, Peter J. *Heroes of the City of Man*. Moscow, ID: Canon Press, 1999.

Leithart, Peter J. *Solomon Among the Postmoderns*. Grand Rapids: Brazos, 2008.

Leithart, Peter J. *Defending Constantine*. Downers Grove, IL: IVP, 2010.

Leithart, Peter J. *Deep Comedy*. Moscow, ID: Canon Press, 2011.

Leithart, Peter J. *Between Babel and Beast*. Eugene, OR: Cascade, 2012.

Leithart, Peter J. *Shining Glory: Reflections on Terrence Malick's Tree of Life*. Eugene, OR: Cascade, 2013.

Leithart, Peter J. *Gratitude: An Intellectual History*. Waco, TX: Baylor, 2014.

Leithart, Peter J. *Traces of the Trinity*. Grand Rapids: Brazos, 2016.

Roberts, Alastair. *Heirs Together: A Theology of the Sexes*. Crossway, 2019.

CPSIA information can be obtained
at www.ICGtesting.com
Printed in the USA
FSHW011023020721
82810FS

9 781733 535649